The St. Louis African American Community and the Exodusters

The St. Louis African American Community and the Exodusters

Bryan M. Jack

University of Missouri Press
Columbia

University of Missouri Press, Columbia, Missouri 65211
Printed and bound in the United States of America

First paperback printing, 2021

Library of Congress Cataloging-in-Publication Data

Jack, Bryan M., 1969–

The St. Louis African American community and the Exodusters / Bryan M. Jack.
p. cm.
Summary: "A story of former slaves searching for their own promised land after the Civil War. Fleeing the South, and trying to reach Kansas, many became stranded in St. Louis. Jack tells how the city's African American community provided food, shelter, and funds to help the Exodusters complete their journey"—Provided by publisher.

Includes bibliographical references and index.
ISBN: 978-0-8262-2237-4 (paperback : alk. paper)
ISBN: 978-0-8262-1772-1 (hard cover : alk. paper)
1. African Americans—Missouri—Saint Louis—History—19th century. 2. Freedmen—West (U.S.)—History—19th century. 3. African American pioneers—West (U.S.)—History—19th century. 4. African Americans—Migrations—History—19th century. 5. Migration, Internal—United States—History—19th century. 6. African Americans—History—1877–1964. 7. Saint Louis (Mo.)—History—19th century. 8. Community life—Missouri—Saint Louis—History—19th century. 9. Saint Louis (Mo.)—Social conditions—19th century. I. Title. II. Title: Saint Louis African American community and the Exodusters.

F474.S29N437 2007
977.8'6600496073—dc22

2007039945

♾ This paper meets the requirements of the American National Standard for Permanence of Paper for Printed Library Materials, Z39.48, 1984.

Designer: Stephanie Foley
Typefaces: Adobe Garamond and ITC Fenice

For Mom

CONTENTS

ACKNOWLEDGMENTS

This book began as a paper in a graduate class at Saint Louis University; it then grew to a dissertation, and finally into the book that you are holding. However, my interest in the Exodusters was formed in high school. My hometown of Parsons, Kansas, sits in the southeast corner of the state, not far from both the Missouri and Oklahoma state lines. A few years after its founding as a stop on the Missouri, Kansas and Texas railroad, Parsons became the first stop for many Exodusters from Texas. Many of these Exodusters stayed in the area, leading to a vibrant African American community in Parsons. The story of the Exodusters landing in Parsons was familiar to me as I was growing up; graduate school gave me the opportunity to explore the Exodusters from a slightly different angle. As my research began in earnest, I learned that St. Louis had played an important role in the movement and was an important story that had yet to be told. Although I haven't lived in Parsons for nearly twenty years, I still feel a connection with the area and I'm thankful that my research is related somewhat to my hometown.

No matter how solitary the pursuit of writing history might seem, no one does it alone. I first would like to thank everyone at the University of Missouri Press. Clair Willcox first saw the promise of the topic and was instrumental in guiding me through the process of proposing the manuscript. Beverly Jarrett, Jane Lago, and everyone else offered insightful suggestions that really improved the book. John Brenner was an insightful and effective editor. My research was also a result of help from a variety of sources. Thank you to the staffs at the following libraries: Saint Louis University, Washington University in St. Louis, the Jefferson Library and Mercantile Library at the University of Missouri–St. Louis,

St. Louis Community College at Meramec, the University of Kansas, Winston-Salem State University, the University of North Carolina–Greensboro, St. Louis City Public Library, the Bancroft Library, and the University of North Carolina. Additionally, I would like to thank the staffs at the following research centers: the Missouri Historical Society, the State Historical Society of Missouri, the Kansas Historical Society, the Western Historical Manuscript Collection, University of Missouri–St. Louis, and the Library of Congress. I would also like to thank fellow scholars Lawrence Christensen, Quintard Taylor, Kimberly Phillips, and Diane Mutti-Burke for their comments; a better book resulted from their input. Thanks also go to Nell Irvin Painter and Heather Cox Richardson for their generosity in answering my questions.

I was fortunate to be taught by outstanding and caring professors throughout my life as a student and into my life as a historian. Karen Exon at Baker University has been a valuable mentor since my undergraduate days. Her personal touch epitomizes what Baker is all about. The American Studies faculty at the University of Alabama went out of their way to help me and every other new graduate student navigate the sometimes treacherous waters of academia. I especially want to thank Rich Megraw, who was my professor and mentor, and who I am proud to call my friend. It was "Doc" Megraw who convinced me that I could make a life as a historian, and he has been my model for everything that a professor should be. He taught me to take the subject of history seriously, without taking myself too seriously. At Saint Louis University, Shirley Loui took a chance on me, and for that I am forever grateful. Elizabeth Kolmer, Lawrence Barmann, and Matt Mancini were a dream dissertation committee. They were critical but encouraging, and were instrumental in guiding me through the ideas that would become the heart of this book. They each have the amazing ability to make each student feel like they are the most important student in the program, and I am proud to have graduated from the department. They continue to remain important voices in my life.

My colleagues in the Department of Social Sciences at Winston-Salem State University have been very encouraging. Our diverse department of historians, sociologists, psychologists, philosophers, geographers, political scientists, and gerontologists, although based in such widely varied disciplines, still manage to support each other in our various pursuits. Their words were always encouraging, and I thank them for picking up some of the slack when I was absorbed in finishing this project. I would also like to thank my students, who liked seeing me writing and researching as I was assigning them research and writing projects. They have been a continual source of energy, and kept me honest as they would ask when the book was going to be finished.

I have been privileged throughout my life to have close friends. Although most are outside the academic community, our relationships have helped me complete this project. JC, Lance, and Bill throughout twenty years of friendship have continually kept me laughing. Gooding, Billy, Jesse Rich, the BU brothers, Paula Savarino, Maureen Murphy, Rob Lee, Mark and Melinda Cisneros, Kenny and Linda Simpson, Greg Koch, Brian Simpson and Diane Pisacreta, Michael and Shawn Kim, Anand and Suj Palagiri, Ashok Palagiri, Doug and Shannon Gifford, Bubba and Daphne Flores, and Jennifer and Grant Patterson all have helped this project, whether they realize it or not.

My family has been incredibly supportive throughout my entire life in whatever I chose to do. My aunts, uncles, and cousins took an interest in my research and would even send me material when they found it; that kind of helpfulness and care is immeasurable. I feel so lucky to have been raised by my parents, Bill and Dee Jack. From them, I learned a love for history, a sense of place, and a respect for education. This couple who were married as teenagers without a penny to their names raised two educators and a judge; they were remarkable parents. I also feel fortunate that after my Mom passed away my Dad found Linda, a wonderful person and even better stepmother. My brother Jeffry and his wife, Susan, my sister Lori and her husband, Jon, always gave me freedom to be myself, but were always there to pick me up when I fell. They have proudly followed the progress of this project, as I have proudly followed their lives. I've watched Amanda, Erin, Elyse, Alex, and Claire grow from babies to impressive young adults; I'm excited to see what their futures hold. My in-laws, John and Vilma Phillips, Dominic Deyto, and Ninang and Dan Frey, generously made me a part of their family; thank you for everything. Finally, my wife, Jenny, a note card writer without peer, has lived with this project from the beginning and has never once complained about the times it has taken me away. Thank you for your love, patience, faith, and support. I sincerely could not have done it without you.

The St. Louis African American Community and the Exodusters

1

Escape

I think I am too good a man to stay down there and be killed, and don't intend to do it.
—JACOB STEVENS, EXODUSTER

George Rogers, a hard-working sharecropper with little to show for it, had lived a difficult life. By 1879, when Rogers was thirty years old, he had experienced the worst that America had to offer—slavery, terror, and grinding poverty. After years spent toiling in the Southern cotton fields, with his body bent under a blazing sun, Rogers was only further in debt. For some, such hopelessness would lead to both calloused hands and a calloused heart. George Rogers did feel frustration, but remarkably, he also felt hope—hope that he could still give his children a chance at a better life. More than anything else, though, he felt fear.

In the previous decade, Rogers, from Madison Parish, Louisiana, had witnessed groups of white ruffians (commonly known as bulldozers) and night riders terrorizing and murdering other African Americans, and he feared they might kill him as well. Once, in nearby Franklin Parish, Rogers had seen the mutilated body of an eighteen-year-old victim of mob violence. Coming upon the scene the morning after the murder, Rogers spoke with the young man's mother and learned that as many as thirty men had targeted their victim for "being a smart boy" who read newspapers. The mob, dressed in Ku Klux Klan attire, invaded the woman's home, grabbed her son, and, ignoring the mother's cries, shot him in cold blood. They moved back outside, leaving him to die, but the young man did not die immediately; the pain and shock from his wounds caused him to moan and cry out. Unable to comfort her son, his mother begged him to keep silent so that his cries would not draw the attention of the mob. Unfortunately, the young man continued to loudly moan, and the mob eventually heard his voice and burst through the door to finish the job. Years later, the scene was still vivid in George Rogers's mind: they "shot him and shot him all to pieces and made sure of it."[1]

After witnessing further violent acts, and hearing rumors of more to come, Rogers began fearing for his own life, and the lives of his wife and three children. To escape, he joined approximately fifty other people and boarded a northern-bound boat to ride the Mississippi River out of Louisiana to safety. Kansas was his ultimate goal; he had heard that Kansas was a fertile land that would allow him to support his family in safety and give his children a chance at a future. African Americans who left the South for Kansas in the spring and summer of 1879 were known as Exodusters, their name derived from the biblical story that spoke of escape from oppression and slavery. Like many Exodusters, George Rogers had only enough money to pay his riverboat passage to St. Louis; to complete his journey he was going to need help. In St. Louis, he would find it as the St. Louis African American community organized to support his and others' attempts to start a new life. This community, its role in aiding the Exodus during its most intense period in the spring of 1879, and how that role contributed to the securing of African American freedom, are the focus of this study.[2]

Unfortunately, George Rogers's story was not unique; many people told similar stories of violence and intimidation, experienced in person or learned through third parties. African Americans had been trickling out of the South for years, but in the spring of 1879, thousands began leaving at once. In some areas, the movement had been growing since the end of 1878; by early 1879, it was a reality. The Exodusters were convinced that their movement would be successful, even in the face of

1. Testimony of Charlton H. Tandy, U.S. Senate, Report and Testimony of the *Select Committee of the United States Senate to Investigate the Causes of the Removal of the Negroes from the Southern States to the Northern States,* 46th Cong., 2nd sess., April 5, 1880, pt. 2, 44–45. (Hereinafter referred to as the Voorhees Committee Report.)

2. Voorhees Committee Report, 44–45.

inadequate funds and lack of preparation or leadership. Without a Moses to lead the escape en masse, the migration instead was more personal, as individuals, families, and small groups made decisions about when, where, and how to leave. One Exoduster expressed the common sentiment that "every black man is his own Moses in this exodus." In spite of the lack of planning and organization, the Exodusters' objective was consistently uniform, as nearly all Exodusters set their sights on Kansas, a land that came to represent freedom to the migrants. Inducements to return to the South, deprivation, and observers' warnings of hardships failed to convince the Exodusters to give up their migration.[3]

The reasons that people gave for leaving the South during the Exodus of 1879 typically fell into three categories: lack of personal safety, lack of political opportunity, and lack of economic opportunity. Related and overlapping, these reasons were evident as Southern landowners exploited African American sharecroppers, threatened them with violence if they reacted, and used violence to maintain control of the political and judicial systems. Threats and violence directed at politically active African American Republicans guaranteed white Democratic Redeemer domination of the Southern political system. Violence directed at nonpolitical African Americans served as a warning to everyone that whites would stop at nothing to ensure domination of life in the post-slavery South.[4]

As George Rogers's story illustrates, bulldozers viewed as threats any African Americans who were challenging the system by becoming better informed; thus the killing of the young man for being a "smart boy" who dared to read newspapers. As Reconstruction ended and hopes of creating a racially moderate society became more distant, the system of white supremacy in the South became more overt. This "tri-partite system of social, political, and economic domination" (as Aldon Morris defines it) remained in place until the modern civil rights movement of the 1950s and 1960s, and left many African Americans like George Rogers with the feeling that escape from the South was their only option. If they remained in the South, they feared that the neoslavery of the sharecropping and tenant system would engulf them, or, even worse,

3. Nell Irvin Painter, *Exodusters: Black Migration to Kansas after Reconstruction,* 184–88; James B. Runnion, "The Negro Exodus," 228; *New York Times,* April 7, 1879.

4. Voorhees Committee Report, 65.

that the chattel slave system would be reinstated and reenslavement would follow. African Americans had been living with bulldozing and violence for several years, and had suffered under slavery before that. As white Redeemers gained an even tighter hold on Southern areas, a future that threatened even worse oppression sparked a desire in many blacks to leave.[5]

Their fears of exploitation had foundation. A. G. Horn, editor of the Meridian, Mississippi, *Mercury,* spelled out many Redeemers' goals toward African Americans. Horn wrote, "We would like to engrave a prophecy on stone, to be read by generations in the future. The Negroes in these states will be slaves again or cease to be. Their sole refuge from extinction will be in slavery to the white man." Orange Pucket, a sharecropper who joined the Exodus, spoke of the fear of reenslavement when he stated, "there is a general talk among the whites and colored people, that Jeff Davis will run for President of the Southern States; and the colored people are afraid that they will be made slaves again." Although such a development might sound outlandish to modern ears, for a group of people for whom reading the newspapers was a life-and-death matter, it was a very real fear. For Pucket, such a scenario felt especially likely because he had witnessed white planters' attempts to control the African American population by controlling their mobility. He stated, "They are already trying to prevent their going from one plantation to another without a pass. They tell us that we must submit to it or they will make us do so with muskets." To further illustrate the point that his freedom was tenuous and threatened by whites, when Pucket left for Kansas, a white planter "shook his fist in my face, and said, 'Damn you, sir, you are my property'" before Pucket escaped.[6]

Fortunately, some of the Exodusters' stories are available to us through newspaper interviews and sworn affidavits given while they were on their journey or shortly after they reached Kansas. In St. Louis, relief leaders provided a notary public to take Exoduster statements that were

5. Aldon Morris, "A Retrospective on the Civil Rights Movement: Political and Intellectual Landmarks," 518; Painter, *Exodusters,* 192–93.

6. Laura Haviland, *A Woman's Life-Work,* 490; "Negro Exodus: Report of Col. Frank H. Fletcher, Agent Appointed by the St. Louis Commission to Visit Kansas for the Purpose of Obtaining Information in Regard to Colored Emigration," 19–20. (Hereinafter referred to as the Fletcher Report.)

later introduced into congressional testimony. The St. Louis Commission sent Colonel Frank Fletcher to Kansas to report on the condition of the Exodusters; in doing so, Fletcher conducted interviews with the migrants. Laura Haviland, a Quaker and former abolitionist who led Exoduster relief efforts in Kansas, conducted interviews with Exodusters as well.

Unfortunately, owing to the attitudes of the period, the overwhelming majority of these recorded sources were male. The Exodus of 1879 was primarily a movement of families—men, women, children, old people, and young people were all fleeing the South. One Exoduster was asked why so many old people were making a trip in which they would be more of a burden than a help. He explained that if their fathers and mothers were left behind in the South, they would be killed. In spite of the variety of ages and the presence of both genders, it was the adult men who were speaking for the movement in the affidavits and the interviews, leaving the women and children seemingly silent. However, groups that may seem silent often are not. Building on the work of Elsa Barkley Brown, Robin DG Kelley notes that the family is a central institution of political ideological formation. Although only men were allowed to vote, women and even children had their say as "newly emancipated African Americans viewed the franchise as the collective property of the whole family." Consequently, Kelley argues, "households hold the key to understanding particular episodes of black working-class resistance."[7]

The Exodus of 1879 was an archetypal example of working-class resistance, and it is reasonable to assume that the families "owned" their migration similar to how they "owned" the franchise of their men. Although most of the voices that we are hearing are male, the thoughts and hopes that they are expressing are collective. However, not all of the voices we are hearing are male. One example of a female Exoduster speaking for the group occurred on the St. Louis riverfront early in the migration. When a reporter informed a group of Exodusters that they were mistaken to expect government help of free transportation, land, and mules, and then asked them if they would soon be returning South,

7. Haviland, *A Woman's Life-Work,* 506; Robin DG Kelley, "We Are Not What We Seem: Rethinking Black Working-Class Opposition in the Jim Crow South," 82.

a woman holding a baby immediately replied loudly and clearly, "What, go back! Oh, no; I'd sooner starve here!"[8]

The woman who was quoted was stating the same sentiment that the numerous men who were quoted elsewhere expressed, that she would just as soon die in freedom than submit to reenslavement. Another example of how women took ownership of the migration appears in Frank Fletcher's report on the condition of the Exodusters. Fletcher notes that when Southern landowners sent men to Kansas to persuade the Exodusters to return home (and promised to pay their passage back to the South) it was "the women who drove them off." The interviews, affidavits, and other sources allow, in many ways, the Exodusters to speak for themselves. Their voices will help us to better understand the motivations that would make thousands of people leave their homes with little more than the clothes on their backs and endure an arduous flight to a land that most of them had never seen.[9]

Charlton Tandy spoke with many of the female Exodusters as they passed through St. Louis. Although he did not obtain affidavits from them, he later testified to Congress that in talking to the women he learned that the threat of sexual exploitation was a fact of life for many African American women in the South. Echoing the Cult of True Womanhood which held that purity of body was the female ideal, Tandy testified that African American women "were desirous of being virtuous and living a pure life, for they regarded their virtue just as much as the Anglo-Saxon did, and they wanted to rear their children up—their girls—to live a virtuous and industrious life." However, their purity was threatened because they were often the victims of sexual abuse at the hands of white men. He continued, "If they [white men] saw a likely, intelligent, and buxom colored girl, these men would have them, and it has become innate to pursue that course in having negro women, and they said to me that while they were desirous of being virtuous and all that kind of thing, that yet they were overawed with fear with these men." The proof of the years of sexual exploitation was written, in Tandy's opinion, in faces all across the South. He stated, "And it is plain to every one's eyes that if you go South, you can see them there ring-streaked like the cattle in olden times, by the thou-

8. *St. Louis Globe-Democrat,* March 14, 1879.

9. Fletcher Report, 10–20.

sand."[10] In graphic testimony, Tandy related gruesome stories of violence against African American women in the South. One female Exoduster stated to Tandy and other witnesses that bulldozers had taken her baby from her arms and dashed its head against a tree, killing it. When asked for proof, the woman showed Tandy the blood of her child that stained the apron she still wore. Tandy later told a story related to him by Exodusters from Grand Gulf, in Warren County, Mississippi. A force of thirty white men went to the house of an Exoduster to lynch him before he could leave for Kansas, but the man escaped. In retribution, the bulldozers lynched the man's pregnant wife, hanging her from a nearby tree and crushing the baby that was delivered as she died. The violent experiences that they had lived or heard about convinced many Exodusters to leave the South.[11]

Historians and sociologists often describe migration of people from one area to another through a theory known as "push-pull." In short, this theory holds that "push" factors compel people to leave an area while "pull" factors help determine migrants' intended destination. These push-pull reasons are not always equal. People may have few reasons for leaving their homes but still leave because they are pulled by strong forces in their destination. Conversely, people might have significant push factors causing them to leave and give little thought to where they land. During the Exodus of 1879, the push factors were the social, political, and economic subjugation that African Americans faced in the South. Pull factors included Kansas's reputation as a "free state" before the Civil War (especially as the home of John Brown), the opportunity for land ownership that Exodusters thought Kansas provided, previous African American migration to Kansas, and words of encouragement from Kansas officials.[12]

The Exodusters had numerous valid reasons for leaving the South, but for most it was not just a headlong rush to go anywhere else. True, they were fleeing the South, but they also were specifically going to Kansas. Some Exodusters accepted offers of jobs from Iowa, Nebraska, Minnesota, and other plains states, but most Exodusters turned down these opportunities to instead settle in Kansas. The Exodusters perceived

10. Voorhees Committee Report, pt. 2, 67.
11. Ibid., 68; *New York Times,* April 24, 1879.
12. Rev. J. C. Hartzell, "The Negro Exodus," 727.

opportunity and equality in Kansas while simultaneously needing an avenue of escape from the South. Kansas, and the hope that it offered, became a lifeline for the Exodusters.[13]

Every migrant to the North had their own story to tell. Elder Perry Bradley, a traveling preacher from Mississippi, did not leave the South in the Exodus of 1879, but waited and left the next year instead. However, his compelling story still helps explain the terrors that African Americans faced in the South. Bradley's sermons gained the notice of bulldozers on April 15, 1879, during the Exodus. On that day, Bradley was preaching at a school in Hillsboro, and preached the morning service without incident. However, that night, a gang of armed men dragged him from his night service and pulled him into the woods. The gang did not attempt to conceal their identities. According to Bradley, the leader warned him to quit connecting Christianity with African American liberation, a popular theme of preachers in the wake of emancipation. When Bradley refused, the torture began. Stripping him of his clothing, the mob forced the preacher to lie facedown on the ground, as men tied each of his hands and feet to a stake. Standing on either side of him, two men with whips alternated turns until Bradley had received two hundred lashes, leaving his back permanently scarred. With Bradley feeling too weak and trembling to stand, the bulldozers then switched their focus from religion to politics, ordering him to preach the Democratic doctrine and vote the Democratic ticket. Bradley again refused, and the bulldozers told him to return home with the threat that if he did not "behave himself" the two hundred lashes would be considered a "light brushing" compared to his next punishment.[14]

A few weeks later, after he had recovered from his ordeal, Bradley was back preaching the same themes of liberation and uplift that had first attracted the bulldozers' attention. After a few uneventful sermons, the same group of bulldozers again captured him, but this time their intention was to hang him. Fortunately for Bradley, he was able to escape and hide in the woods. After hiding, Bradley gathered his family and made way for Kansas, where, in his words, he could "vote as well as

13. Voorhees Committee Report, pt. 2, 300; *St. Louis Globe-Democrat,* April 17, 26, 1879.

14. Haviland, *A Woman's Life-Work,* 484–85.

preach according to the dictates of my own conscience without the torturing whip or the hangman's rope."[15]

Political control was a primary goal of the bulldozers, and political freedom was a motivation of the Exodusters. Throughout Reconstruction, there had been political violence perpetrated against African Americans, and the Compromise of 1877 ensured that federal troops had left the South, leaving African Americans even more vulnerable to organized political violence. However, even before the compromise, federal troops had not been able to completely quell the violence. Political considerations, a lack of sufficient troops, and the organization of the anti-black and anti-Republican forces all contributed to the failure to protect African American rights. In examining Mississippi and Louisiana, Nicholas Lemann has argued that this "last battle of the Civil War" ensured white domination of the post-Reconstruction South.[16]

Much of the violence occurred in the same Mississippi counties and Louisiana parishes that would, within the decade, be the epicenter of the Exodus. General Philip Sheridan, military commander of Louisiana and Texas during Reconstruction, reported on the political violence in Louisiana. In 1875, four years before the Exodus, Sheridan noted that in the previous ten years there had been more than 3,500 people killed and wounded across the state. More than 1,200 of these victims had been attacked for political reasons. Sheridan went on to note that the great majority of the victims had been African Americans, and except in a few isolated cases, justice had not been served as arrests and convictions were rare and official governmental investigation was nonexistent.[17]

The 1876 election had been particularly damaging to African American Republicans in Louisiana, and on December 6, 1876, President Ulysses S. Grant sent a ninety-eight-page report to Congress listing more than 4,000 victims of political violence. Republican senators determined that even though Republicans enjoyed a majority of more than 25,000 registered voters on the day of the election, political violence had ensured Democratic domination of Louisiana. They noted, "In fifteen parishes where 17,726 Republicans were registered in 1876 only 5,758 votes were cast for Hayes and Wheeler, and in one of them (East

15. Ibid., 484–85.
16. Nicholas Lemann, *Redemption: The Last Battle of the Civil War,* 176–80.
17. Voorhees Committee Report, pt. 1, 18.

Feliciana) where there were 2,127 Republicans registered but 1 Republican vote was cast. By such methods the Republican majority of the State was supposed to have been effectually suppressed and a Democratic victory assured."[18]

Exoduster John Massey spoke of Mississippi's similar situation. He stated, "On election days we were compelled to vote the Democratic ticket; they would come to us and give us a ticket, and told us if we didn't vote it they would kill us. Times were getting so bad that a colored man dare not speak above his breath for fear of being killed; it was impossible for us to vote the Republican ticket." William Jones, an Exoduster from Warren County, Mississippi, reported that the bulldozers made lethal and indiscriminate use of their guns during elections. He states, "When we got out of the court-house the white people were out in the streets with their needle guns, and were shooting at all the colored people they saw." The bulldozers were not just a few unorganized men who were mobbing their neighbors, but rather were armed and organized troops. Lemann notes that the bulldozers were "well-financed terrorists" armed with the latest military technology. Often, the bulldozers were Confederate veterans, who used military tactics and weaponry (including cannons) to intimidate and control African Americans and their white allies.[19]

Although Democrats attempted to label the bulldozers as renegades who were only operating on local levels, there were close ties to Democratic leaders. Professing their innocence, Democrat leaders claimed to have no control over the bulldozers. Yet, when they wanted the violence to stop for fear of bringing a federal response, it stopped, and when suppressing the African American vote allowed a Democratic victory, it resumed. Democratic leaders were in regular contact with bulldozers all over Mississippi, and used them as a military arm of the Democratic Party. The tactic was effective, as the bulldozers disenfranchised African Americans all across the state. In some counties during the 1875 state elections, not a single Republican vote was cast. In one example of the effectiveness of the political terrorism, Yazoo County's African American population of twelve thousand cast only seven Republican votes.[20]

18. Arvarh E. Strickland, "Toward the Promised Land: The Exodus to Kansas and Afterword," 393; Voorhees Committee Report, pt. 1, 19.

19. Voorhees Committee Report, pt. 2, 56–62; Lemann, *Redemption,* 76, 147.

20. Ibid., 127–54.

J. D. Daniel, a forty-five-year-old sharecropper from Warren County, Mississippi, reported that even when African Americans could vote as they wished, their votes often went uncounted. In 1874, five years before the Exodus, African Americans in his district had held a meeting to teach each other how to vote, and all voted the Republican ticket. At gunpoint, the Democrats stole the ballot box and threw it in the river. From that time forward, whites controlled the voting in Warren County. In Louisiana, the tactics were similar. Clarence Winn, an Exoduster from Madison Parish, stated that at Ravia, a polling station in Morehouse Parish, "25 or 30 men burst in the doors and took the ballots and would have killed the colored men—H. W. Jackson, Nathan Brooks and H. P. Palmer—who had charge of the ballot-boxes, if they could have caught them; but they ran off."[21]

According to the Exodusters, even after Redemption African Americans did not surrender. Many insisted on exerting their quickly diminishing political rights. With no risk of federal intervention, and with carte blanche to do as they wished, whites continued to resort to violence. Emile Auspitz, a traveling peddler who joined the Exodus, reported that in his travels throughout Louisiana and Texas he had witnessed numerous cases of political intimidation. He testified that white bulldozers waited at many polling places with guns cocked to intimidate African American voters. T. J. Watts, a saloon-keeper from Vicksburg, reported that the Democrats in that city would not even allow the Republicans to nominate a ticket for the local city elections in 1878.[22]

This disenfranchisement of African Americans in the South was not unknown to federal officials. In 1878, President Rutherford B. Hayes wrote in his diary, "By state legislation, by frauds, by intimidation, and by violence of the most atrocious character, colored citizens have been deprived of the right of suffrage—a right guaranteed by the Constitution, and to the protection of which the people of these states have solemnly pledged." Although frustrated by the actions of Southern Redeemers, Hayes and other leaders were reluctant to risk widening the rift between North and South to protect African American rights. Instead, the South was left to its own devices, meaning that white supremacy would be allowed to grow to maintain national unity. As Northern leaders attempted to keep the Civil War in the past, Southern whites

21. Vorhees Committee Report, pt. 2, 46–50.
22. Ibid., 52–54.

worked to build a society that was as close to the antebellum racial caste system as possible. For the Exodusters, who recognized a worsening situation and a threatening future, the options became clear: they could stay put and submit, or leave.[23]

Henry Dethloff and Robert Jones examined race relations in Louisiana from 1877 to 1898 and determined that until 1898, African Americans were able to maintain political influence and participate in the political process on many levels, including "voting, holding state and political offices, receiving Federal and state patronage, and participating in party conventions and councils." To the authors, the evidence that they found essentially confirmed C. Vann Woodward's thesis that milder alternatives to segregation were available and practiced in the 1870s and 1880s. According to Woodward, it was not until the late 1890s when white Southerners imposed a system of "consistent, thorough, and legally sanctioned segregation" that subjugation was complete.[24]

The promise and flexibility of 1870s Louisiana observed by Woodward, Dethloff, and Jones seem to argue against the Exodusters' claims of near total suppression. However, according to Dethloff and Jones, the degree to which an African American "could exercise his political, social, and civil rights depended upon a wide range of circumstances," including racial discrimination. Additionally, they note, "the most striking aspect of race relations in Louisiana from 1877–1898 was the absence of a system. There existed no consistent, thorough, and effective system of social control, legal or extralegal, governing relations between the races." Instead, the system was fluid, and no clear statewide definition of the relationships between white and African American citizens was yet determined. In the rural, heavily African American, alluvial parishes along the Mississippi River, this definition was being written in the 1870s. As Nell Irvin Painter reminds us, seven Louisiana parishes (including the Exoduster parishes of Madison, Tensas, Ouachita, and Concordia) "witnessed lawlessness and election irregularities in 1878" as Democrats isolated African American Republicans. This violence even

23. Kenneth E. Davison, *The Presidency of Rutherford B. Hayes,* 142–43; Painter, *Exodusters,* 180.

24. Donald G. Nieman, ed., *African Americans and the Emergence of Segregation 1865–1900,* 68–69.

spilled across the Mississippi River to affect Mississippi counties that would also contribute to the Exodus.[25]

The Exodusters saw many of the gains made during the early years of Reconstruction disappear in the face of white resistance. People were afraid of losing their rights, and even more fundamentally, they were afraid of losing their lives. Morgan Peoples argues that they were reasonable in their fear, as at least thirty people were killed during the election of 1878 in Louisiana. As tales (some true and some likely exaggerated) of these and other killings spread, the idea of leaving the South became increasingly important for thousands of African Americans. Squire Hughes, an Exoduster from near Vicksburg, Mississippi, understood the importance of credibly relating what was happening in the South by stating, "I saw nine [bodies] put in one pile, that had been killed, and the colored people had to bury them; eight others were found killed in the woods. I know that. I have heard about other killings; but I know about these." Many other Exodusters recounted stories of political violence. It is important to keep in mind that whether the violence was experienced firsthand or heard as a rumor is of somewhat secondary importance. As a catalyst for the Exodus, what is important is that the Exodusters believed it to be true and acted upon it by escaping to Kansas.[26]

One Exoduster reported to Frank Fletcher the frustration felt by the overwhelmingly Republican African American population in the post-Reconstruction South. He stated, "Four of them came to my house with guns cocked to prevent my voting last fall. They tell us, 'If we can't out-vote you, we'll out-count you; and if we can't out-count you, we'll out shoot you.' I verily believe that many a colored man will be killed next election. If a colored man stays away from the polls and does not vote, they spot him, and make him vote. If he votes their way, they treat him no better in business. They hire the colored people to vote, and then take their pay away." The *St. Louis Globe-Democrat* reported a similar story from an Exoduster. The paper reported, "If a 'nigger' did not vote the Democratic ticket, he had better not vote at all, or he was spoilt meat in a few days. A 'nigger' could not rent land or work at all who did not vote with the white man. The Democrats put the ballots

25. Ibid., 69; Painter, *Exodusters,* 160–62.

26. Morgan Peoples, "'Kansas Fever' in North Louisiana," 125; Fletcher Report, 14.

into their hands, in their houses, in the fields, in the streets. The only alternative was a Democratic ballot or a Democratic bullet." Another alternative, of course, was to leave for Kansas, an option taken by many people.[27]

Southern white society had always held African American rights in low regard, but after the passage of the Fifteenth Amendment made African Americans a political threat to white domination, the South became increasingly unsafe for African Americans and their allies. Richard Coutcher, a farmer from Hinds County, Mississippi, joined four other families in leaving the state. In Kansas, he told Frank Fletcher, "I knew colored men killed because they were Republicans. The colored people have got so that they are afraid of their lives to live there . . . The white people have sworn they will kill the last one of us if we don't vote with them, and they were killing us so fast, I thought I would get away while I could." A woman from his party spoke of similar fears, but was more specific. She stated that her white landlord had told her husband, "John, I've asked you to vote with us a good many times, and I don't intend to do it again." Since the whites had previously stated that they would kill all the Republicans, her husband took this statement as a warning and a threat to his life. He had good foundation to feel fear as local whites had recently killed eleven members of a family named Page. After many nights of the Exoduster family being chased from their beds, they sold their corn, left four horses behind, and fled to Kansas. Despite the difficulties of the trip, the woman stated, "I am better off up here, if I don't get a piece of meat but once a day. I can lay down at night and I ain't afraid. Some of them is in a worse condition down South than they was when they was when slaves." Frederick Marshall, a fifty-three-year-old sharecropper from Natchez, confirmed the woman's account of the Page killings; he was a witness. Marshall said that he had watched a group of fifteen or twenty white men kill Page for being "one of the smart men." After witnessing the killing, Marshall was constantly in fear for his life. He and his wife left for Kansas because, in his words, "I had to go someplace where I could work without being afraid of my life."[28]

27. Fletcher Report, 19; *St. Louis Globe-Democrat,* March 12, 1879.
28. Fletcher Report, 6; Voorhees Committee Report, pt. 2, 53–54.

James Brown, a thirty-year-old sharecropper from Madison Parish, Louisiana, also left the South because he did not have the right to vote as he wanted. Like most Exodusters, Brown's economic status as a sharecropper made him particularly vulnerable, because he could be threatened both physically and economically. His landlord Mr. Bradley told him, "Brown, by God, if you go to the polls I want you to cast the right ticket." When Brown feigned ignorance and asked which ticket Bradley meant, Bradley replied, "Jim, we are going to carry this thing our way, you God damn niggers have had this thing your own way long enough, and we white folks are going to have it our own way or kill out all you God damn Republican niggers." When Brown heard the (false) rumor that the federal government and the railroads were promising free transportation to Kansas from St. Louis, and that land in Kansas was available on five-year payments, he packed up his family and left. Although the false promise of free land and transportation left Brown, his wife, and mother-in-law stranded in St. Louis with their eight children, Brown remained adamant that he "would never go South again," a feeling shared by most Exodusters.[29]

Jacob Stevens, the twenty-two-year-old sharecropper whose words provide the epigraph for this chapter, left Mississippi not after threats, but after personally witnessing the murders of his father and brother. Stevens's story also describes how the violence sometimes reached beyond African Americans to encompass sympathetic whites. Stevens and his brother Ike had been to visit a Mr. Hoffer, a white man who, in Stevens's words, "held in with the black people." Finding Mr. Hoffer murdered by bulldozers, Stevens, his brother, and women from their family had nearly returned home when a group of seventy-five armed white men confronted them. Ike Stevens, who was in the lead, refused to halt when ordered to do so, and was shot dead at such close range that the muzzle flash burned his shirt collar.[30]

The mob then ordered Stevens's father out of the house and began to interrogate him about the Republican club that he belonged to and other Radical Republican activity. When he refused to answer, they marched him down the road, and, over the cries of his wife, killed him, too. The mob wore no disguises, and Jacob Stevens recognized at least

29. Voorhees Committee Report, 49.
30. Ibid., 55–56.

two of the men who participated. Two years after the killing, when Stevens saw things getting worse and not better, he finally left the South. While in St. Louis, he stated, "Couldn't carry me back South again unless they would chain me and carry me back. My people are there, and I would like to see them, but I can't go back."[31]

Another man who lost a brother to the violence was Joseph Fletcher, an honorably discharged soldier who was living in the Red River section of Louisiana. Fletcher claimed to have witnessed "one hundred men killed by shooting and hanging during the two years, 1878 and 1879," noting that his brother was one of the victims. The only crime the victims committed, according to Fletcher, was "their persistence in voting the Republican ticket." After interviewing Fletcher about this incredible number of political murders, Laura Haviland remarked that "a number of the representative men from those parishes were interviewed, and they testified to the same things." To attest to their credibility, Haviland noted that "a number of them had been soldiers."[32]

Haviland reported that African American candidates for political office came under special scrutiny from the bulldozers. Andrew J. Jackson, from the frequently bulldozed area around Waterproof, Mississippi, told her the story of a man named Fairfax, a "smart, educated man" who was a landowner and a major contributor to the colored Baptist Church. After bulldozers burned down his house and the church, Fairfax rebuilt his house and agreed to be the Republican nominee for senator. When the Democrats found out, they threatened his life, but Fairfax escaped to New Orleans. According to Jackson, the Democrats began sending letters and telegrams to Fairfax, telling him to come back and promising not to harm him. Still fearing for his life, Fairfax ignored their requests. Finally, one white man who had always appeared friendly to Fairfax went to New Orleans to promise him that no harm would come to him if he would return to Mississippi to use his influence to convince African Americans to stop leaving for Kansas. Assured of his friend's sincerity, Fairfax returned to Mississippi on a Saturday—and was shot dead before Monday morning. His death guaranteed a Democratic victory in the election.[33]

31. Ibid., 55–56.
32. Haviland, *A Woman's Life-Work,* 496.
33. Ibid., 496–97.

A person did not have to be a Republican candidate to suffer attack; simply attending political speeches, voting, or being an organizer of any kind was dangerous. Daniel Parker was chased out of Louisiana after being elected president of a club that was working to win a reduction in rent from local landowners. After bulldozers threatened his life, Parker headed north; the suddenness of his escape meant leaving his family behind with hopes that they would reunite in Kansas. John Massey of Mississippi spoke of a friend of his, Henry Curtis, who was killed for attending Radical speeches. William Jones reported that in his home county of Warren, Mississippi, he and other African Americans went to the courthouse in the spring of 1878 to vote and to hear speeches, although the county was under Democratic control. As people were listening to the speeches, a crowd of twenty to thirty white Democrats opened fire with pistols, wounding two African Americans. After another year of terror, Jones and his wife packed up their two children and headed to Kansas, with Jones proclaiming, "I never will go back to the South again; I would die first."[34]

It may sound simplistic, but the freedom to gather in groups, to discuss politics, to be informed of events, to run for office, or to vote for any candidate one chooses are freedoms that are at the heart of American democracy. The right to earn a living, protect and provide for one's family, get an education, and own land are all celebrated within American society. The post-Reconstruction South appeared to deny these rights to many African Americans into perpetuity. African Americans in the South rightly believed that denial of their political rights also meant denial of their economic and social rights as well, leading F. R. Guernsey, a British observer, to write, "the discontent of the negro with his merely nominal citizenship in many Southern communities has more to do with the exodus than all else . . . to the impartial observer of affairs in Mississippi and Louisiana it cannot fail to be apparent that the negroes are greatly dissatisfied with their political condition." When asked why poverty-stricken Exodusters would leave the South without proper means, one departing man replied, "That's what white men go to new countries for isn't it? You do not tell them to stay back because they are poor. Who was the Homestead Act made for if it was not for poor men?" As immigrants were landing on the shores of the United

34. Voorhees Committee Report, pt. 2, 51–62.

States, fleeing tyranny and seeking a better life, a similar movement was occurring within the nation as well. Only these were American citizens, simply asking for America to live up to its stated ideals. One Exoduster told an interviewer, "We are an integral part of the American people. You cannot oppress us without doing violence to yourselves."[35]

At the height of the Exodus, the *New York Times* explained to its readers what was causing the migration. In keeping with the masculine emphasis of the day, it noted of the African American in the South, "He is a proscribed man. He has political rights only in theory. Practically, he is not a freeman. So long as he exercises only the humblest rights of a human being, having no opinions concerning the matters which move most men, and confining himself to the meanest cares which can engross the attention of any human being, he is permitted to live unmolested." One African American religious leader in St. Louis stated that African Americans had been exploring migration for years, and believed that the ability to migrate was "the evidence and seal of emancipation." In other words, the ability to move from the South was the mechanism that would both illustrate and guarantee their rights as free Americans.[36]

If their rights were not going to be protected at home, the Exodusters viewed Kansas as a place that would protect their rights and provide them with economic opportunity. One group of Exodusters from Louisiana sent J. H. Cox to Kansas to investigate the situation and help them decide whether to leave. He stated, "The majority prefer Kansas. They have the impression that it is a free State, and always has been. By *free,* I mean a place where they will be allowed to exercise the rights of citizenship." Although some Exodusters were blindly heading into the unknown, others, like the group that utilized Cox, tried to find information about their destination beyond the rampant rumors.[37]

When time, expense, or opportunity made it difficult to send someone to scout out the destination, some Exodusters used other means. During the journey, Frank Fletcher interviewed George Roan, who traveled with fourteen other adults and nine children from Tensas Parish,

35. F. R. Guernsey, "The Negro Exodus," 378–86; Thomas C. Cox, *Blacks in Topeka, Kansas 1865–1915: A Social History,* 41–42.

36. *New York Times,* March 18, 1879; *Nation,* April 10, 1879.

37. Fletcher Report, 15.

Louisiana. Roan discussed how he investigated Kansas before starting his journey. "We were working every day, and getting nothing. We could not do worse anywhere than we were doing there . . . I learned of Kansas from the newspapers that I got hold of. They were Southern papers. I got a map, and found out where Kansas was; and I got a 'History of the United States,' and read about it." Undoubtedly, the history that Roan consulted discussed Kansas's role as a free state before the Civil War, which would help solidify its reputation as a desirable destination. Bulldozers accused Curtis Pollard, a former member of the Louisiana state senate and legislature, of teaching people about Kansas; the threats to his life necessitated his own departure. Pollard reluctantly took credit for starting the exodus in his neighborhood in Madison Parish, Louisiana. He told St. Louis relief leaders, "The talk about going to Kansas where I lived, I supposed, was caused by my getting hold of a couple of maps and showing them to the people. I intend to go to Kansas, to Topeka."[38]

While denied political rights in the South, the Exodusters attempted to maintain another important right—mobility—the right to move. If movement of free people is limited, then freedom itself is limited, because mobility is, as William Cohen argues, "central to the concept of freedom." In his book, *At Freedom's Edge: Black Mobility and the Southern White Quest for Racial Control,* Cohen argues that African Americans continually resisted whites' attempts at immobilizing them. He states, "Deprived of many of the most basic rights of citizenship, they clung tenaciously to that most important of rights, the right to move." By leaving the post-Reconstruction South for a new life on the Kansas plains, the Exodusters were a vibrant example of the lengths that African Americans would go to maintain their hard-won freedom. Thwarting their attempt to move would result in a return, if not to actual slavery, then to seemingly hopeless subjugation. When the *New York Times* wrote in a front-page story in April 1879, that the Exodusters' "struggle to make their way to the free West should receive the attention of liberty-loving men and women everywhere," it illustrated the point that the Kansas Exodus represented more than a simple migration to many observers. The St. Louis African American community became the first

38. Ibid., 19; Voorhees Committee Report, pt. 2, 47–48.

outsiders to recognize the importance of the Exodus. Even more critically, they acted to aid the Exodusters.[39]

The Exodusters, like other Americans, understood that they were not truly free until they had freedom of movement to leave the South. As Cohen writes, "central to slavery had been the ability of the masters to control black movement; central to freedom was the right of former bondsmen to pick up and move where they wished . . . the fifty years after the Civil War were marked by a continuing struggle over how much freedom of movement blacks should have." Many Exodusters rightly believed that post-Reconstruction restrictions on African Americans could threaten their ability to leave the South. Henry Adams voiced the views of many when he stated, "the Democrats, as well as the Slave Holders, of the South will fix it so that we can not get from the South to the North unless we run away, for we Believed that not any colored man will be allowed to Leave the South without a Pass."[40]

Whites tried to control African American mobility through labor contracts and vagrancy laws, and African Americans understood that land ownership was a remedy. To former slaves, who had watched others profit from black labor for generations, freedom was inextricably tied with economic autonomy, which was dependent upon land ownership. However, land ownership in the South was difficult to attain. Like George Rogers, many of the Exodusters in 1879 were sharecroppers; they were fleeing the South, in part, to have the opportunity to profit from their own labor, and to gain the material goods and independence that land ownership provided.[41]

The sharecropping life in the post-Reconstruction South was unbelievably difficult. Jacqueline Jones describes the typical sharecropper's home by writing, "it lacked glass windows, screens to keep out bugs and flies, running water, sanitary facilities, artificial illumination, cupboard and shelf space, and adequate insulation as well as ventilation." In spite of the typical large number of family members, the often one-room cabins meant that all activities occurred in the same space. By

39. William Cohen, *At Freedom's Edge: Black Mobility and the Southern White Quest for Racial Control, 1861–1915,* xii-xvi; *New York Times,* April 3, 1879.

40. Cohen, *At Freedom's Edge,* 3; Painter, *Exodusters,* 193.

41. Eric Foner, *The Story of American Freedom,* 102; *People's Advocate,* September 29, 1879.

sharing eating, bathing, and sleeping space, illnesses were common and privacy was precious. It was not only the physical structure of the cabin that made life difficult for sharecroppers. Additionally, Jones notes, "Sharecroppers' households also lacked artifacts of middle-class life, such as a wide variety of eating and cooking utensils, books, papers, pencils, bric-a-brac, and clocks. Black rural women relied on a very few pieces of basic equipment in the course of the day; these included a large tub in which to bathe the youngsters and scrub the clothes, a cooking kettle, and a water pail." This lack of material goods meant that sharecroppers' "standard of living was considerably lower than that of midcentury western pioneer families." This lower standard of living declined even further as many Exodusters sold their belongings to pay their passage to St. Louis. Although they did not travel with many belongings, the Exodusters did carry with them their stories of economic exploitation.[42]

There were two related labor systems in the South: the sharecrop system and the tenant system. African American farm laborers were often compelled to work within one of these systems. Early after emancipation, many former slaves preferred these systems over plantation-style wage labor because they provided a level of autonomy that wage labor lacked, and they were a form of free labor. As William Cohen notes, "Tenants and sharecroppers both worked individual plots of land, and both divided their crops with the landowner according to the terms of a prearranged contract. But there the similarities ended. Tenants owned the crops they grew, croppers did not." Tenant farming gave the laborer more autonomy, as most sharecropper contracts stipulated that the landowner could supervise nearly all farming activity. Tenants, on the other hand, were free to make decisions about the land they rented. Theoretically, both systems could allow African Americans to work their way toward land ownership as they saved money earned from the crops they produced. In reality, the system often left sharecroppers and tenants deeper in debt as landowners charged exorbitant prices for goods and then claimed more than their share after harvest or during ginning.[43]

42. Jacqueline Jones, *Labor of Love, Labor of Sorrow: Black Women, Work and the Family, from Slavery to the Present,* 86.

43. Cohen, *At Freedom's Edge,* 20–21.

Landowners often blamed sharecroppers' and tenants' economic difficulties on a lack of thrift, as sharecroppers blamed the landowners for exploiting the system in order to keep African American labor tied to the land. A Democratic newspaper in St. Louis that was hostile to the Exodus played into white stereotypes of African Americans when describing the difficulties faced by the sharecroppers. The paper interviewed a Vicksburg landowner, W. W. Gibson, to explain the Exodus. Gibson's explanation was that the sharecroppers were suffering because of their "shortsightedness and improvidence" and their willingness to gamble their money away. He denied any mistreatment of the sharecroppers, and stated that rather than taking advantage of the sharecroppers, the landowners were magnanimous about carrying debt for them.[44]

There was little recourse for sharecroppers who believed that they were cheated—landowners used the courts and law enforcement, or outright violence, to punish sharecroppers who questioned their accounting. Sam Jamison, who traveled north in March of 1879, spoke to a St. Louis reporter of his frustration with the system. Jamison stated, "You see, it's just this way. The colored people couldn't own ground of their own, so they must farm on shares—small farms at that. Well, we would go to work, raise a crop, the owners furnishing everything until the crop was saved. Then came the settlement, and generally what was made was nothing for the darky; all that was swallowed by expenses or at least the owners and overseers pretended." When the reporter asked Jamison about legal recourse that was available, Jamison was contemptuous, saying, "There's no law down there for the colored man. Not even to protect his life, let alone his money."[45]

Likewise, Philip Fauber told Laura Haviland that he was to furnish the team, cottonseed, and labor, and for this outlay expected to receive one third of the cotton crop. He took three bales to the weigher, who set aside the one bale due Fauber according to the contract. When his property owners, the McNealys, claimed all three bales, Fauber turned to the Justice of the Peace, who looked at the contract and indicated that Fauber was due one bale of cotton. The McNealys, unsatisfied with two thirds of the crop, called a different officer who read, then tore up

44. *Missouri Republican,* March 15, 1879.
45. *St. Louis Globe-Democrat,* March 17, 1879.

the contract and awarded the property owners all three bales of cotton. Despite Fauber's begging his property owners not to take away his family's only chance at an income for the winter, the McNealys left with all three bales of cotton. Unfortunately for Fauber, the dispute did not end there. On his way home, he was ambushed in the woods and received a shotgun blast to the face, which permanently blinded him. Although the McNealys denied shooting him, Fauber remained convinced that they at least knew the culprit. In Kansas, Fauber's wife hoped to support them both by farming four or five acres single-handed.[46]

During the Exodus, George Rogers spoke of the lack of economic opportunity that he faced in Louisiana. Rogers, whose story opened this chapter, indicated that in Madison Parish his property owner was the local police official, a Major Lucas. Although Rogers was successful in growing good cotton crops, Lucas would force Rogers to give up the cotton and take it to the gin himself. According to the contract he had to sign, Rogers had no choice in the matter—he had to have the cotton ginned at Lucas's gin. After the ginning, Lucas would keep the cotton and claim that Rogers had not grown enough of it to pay for his rent and the ginning. Consequently, at the end of the year, Rogers would be deeper in debt to Lucas, and would be required to attempt to grow another crop to pay off his debt. Rogers had no recourse to challenge Lucas, who had the legal system and law on his side. In Kansas, however, Rogers hoped to "get his own living."[47]

Henry Jackson, an Exoduster from Louisiana, was in a similar situation. As a seventy-three year old, he had produced ten bales of cotton, but his landowner took it from him, shipped it to market, and kept all of the money. Jackson protested, and eventually sued for his compensation, but was denied. Since he had no money, the landowner tried to convince him to pawn his horse and begin again. Instead, at seventy-five years of age, Jackson sold his horse, bought passage for him and his wife to Kansas, and decided to start over.[48]

Like Sam Jamison, Henry Jackson, and George Rogers, many Exodusters left the South because of fear, but also because of economic reasons. F. R. Guernsey, in investigating the Exodus as it occurred, stated

46. Haviland, *A Woman's Life-Work,* 502.
47. Voorhees Committee Report, pt. 2, 44–45.
48. Ibid., 60.

that the Exodusters were consistent in their claims that white cruelty and exploitation were their reasons for leaving the South. He writes, "Every negro tenant who had brought with him a 'pass book,' or account with the plantation-store, produced his book as indisputable evidence of the rapacity of the whites. . . . Many of these books showed that the Negroes had been charged for the commonest necessaries of life prices often one hundred per cent higher than Northern retail quotations for the same articles. Copies of contracts and leases were shown to corroborate the universal story of exorbitant land-rents."[49]

Charlton Tandy, the first St. Louisan to come to the aid of the Exodusters, and the organizer of St. Louis relief efforts, testified before the Senate on the Exodusters' behalf. Using contracts and account books provided to him by Exodusters, Tandy corroborated Guernsey's findings. He testified that African Americans were charged yearly rent for land at rates nearly equivalent to the land's purchase price. In addition, the materials that African Americans were forced to purchase from the property owners were often marked up two and three times their standard price. For example, Tandy notes, "The price of meal is put down at $2 a bushel, although it has rarely been worth more than $1 even in the summer. Molasses is charged at $1.50 a gallon, for which 75 cents would be a large price, and tobacco at 50 cents a plug (one-third of a pound), which is worth about 60 cents a pound at retail in the country in the Southern States." The contracts that African Americans had to sign not only contained provisions to put African Americans in debt, but also the charge for the contract itself was exorbitant. Tandy stated, "filling out a contract the charge was $2.50. A notary would do the same in New York or New England at a price ranging from 25 cents to $1."[50]

Of course, in the cash-strapped credit culture of the post-Reconstruction South, payment for these products and services was held in a lien against the cotton crop. Tandy notes, "In almost every instance there was a small balance against the colored planter, although if only fair prices had been charged for the provisions a considerable balance would have appeared on the other side of the account." Instead, African Americans, forced into unfair contracts, were often further in debt after a year of hard labor than they had been the year before.[51]

49. Guernsey, "The Negro Exodus," 374.
50. Voorhees Committee Report, pt. 2, 63.
51. Ibid., 63.

The *St. Louis Globe-Democrat,* a Republican paper that was a lukewarm supporter of the Exodus, explained to its readers how the cotton agriculture of the South left the Exodusters with few options. In the Exoduster districts, cotton was king; it was the primary crop, the primary form of payment, and it was profitable when cheap—primarily black—labor was available. The sharecrop system, when combined with white societal control, allowed the landowners to maintain a low-cost labor force. The paper reported that the fertile land would grow anything, but since cotton was most profitable, it was what was grown. According to the paper, the sharecropper never had a chance. It reported, "the storekeeper and the land-owner ascertain how much of it [cotton] he will have, and when it comes settling time they charge the poor fool with just enough to take all his cotton and make him a few dollars in debt. He is poorer after his crop is sold than before." John Lucas, from Warren County, Mississippi, stated that even when he tried to work jobs for cash in addition to sharecropping, he was only paid in scrip. The hopelessness of the situation caused one migrant to exclaim, "We've been working for fourteen long years, and we ain't no better off than we was when we commenced."[52]

The Exodusters hoped that in Kansas, they would find the political, economic, and social freedom that they were seeking. Leaving the South was not an easy decision, but for many, it was necessary. The Exodusters were laborers, and by leaving the South and taking their labor with them, they were exercising the only power that they had. To complete the journey, most Exodusters were going to have to rely on strangers to feed, clothe, and house them, and, more importantly, to help them reach their destination. As they climbed onboard the Mississippi River packet boats and slowly steamed to the promise of a better future, they left both chattel and neo-slavery behind.[53]

52. *St. Louis Globe-Democrat,* March 13, 1879; Fletcher Report, 17; Runnion, "The Negro Exodus," 223.

53. Heather Cox Richardson, *The Death of Reconstruction: Race, Labor, and Politics in the Post–Civil War North, 1865–1901,* 171.

2

Relief

I would not go back to the South again.
Before I would do it I would walk up and
down the streets and pick up the crusts.
— EDWARD PARLOR, EXODUSTER

The Exodusters' journey up the Mississippi River to St. Louis lasted up to eight days, and was an ordeal for many of the travelers. During the spring of 1879, most Exodusters paid four dollars for deck passage that provided little in the way of amenities—the men, women, and children who made the trek to St. Louis supplied their own food and bedding and constructed makeshift shelters to protect themselves from the raw river winds. As they rode on the deck, situated among the containers of freight, their status on the ship reflected their marginalization within society. Chattel slavery (which many of the Exodusters had personally experienced) had denied African Americans humanity by classifying them as property. Now, during their flight from the South, the Exodusters were being classified not as passengers, and not as freight, but as something in between.[1]

Describing the Exodusters' riverboat accommodations, a St. Louis newspaper reporter wrote, "Along the lower guards, on both sides of the boat back to the furnaces, enclosing the space covered above by the cabins, were hung and piled up blankets, quilts, sheets, mattresses, and even spare clothing." The reporter describes the Exodusters as

1. *St. Louis Globe-Democrat,* March 17, 1879; Robert G. Athearn, *In Search of Canaan,* 9.

property, an "ebony-hued cargo, the third consignment of a once valuable commodity." However, the reporter recognized the desperation, and finally the humanity, of the Exodusters, noting that they were "billeted for anywhere out of the limits of Dixie; and it is safe to say that a more disconsolate lot of human beings never occupied the hull of a steamboat."[2]

Upon arrival in St. Louis, the cabin passengers traveled to hotels in waiting cabs and the freight was loaded into warehouses, while the first waves of Exodusters were simply ordered to go ashore into the unknown. Whether their status would improve upon arrival in St. Louis would be largely out of their hands; their well-being would be dependent upon St. Louisans. Unfortunately, the white community of St. Louis, including the city leaders, would at best be ambivalent about the Exodusters and would prove to be hostile to the Exodus. Fortunately for the Exodusters, the St. Louis African American community recognized not only their worth as fellow human beings and fellow African Americans but also the value of their movement out of the South. The community provided the Exodusters with ways to both assert their humanity and complete their journey.[3]

Early in March 1879, a group of 250 Exodusters appeared on the snowy St. Louis wharf, and as they descended the gangplank of the crowded packet boat, they shivered in the cold and damp March air. Carrying their few possessions and unsure of their next step, the men, women, and children braced themselves against the chill. Dressed in tattered, lightweight clothes more appropriate for summer cotton picking than for winter travel, the milling crowd appeared out of place amongst the usual activities of the wharf. The unfamiliar sights and sounds of St. Louis frightened the rural Southern migrants, but the group gave no indication of wanting to return home. Instead, the travelers displayed a faith that everything was going to be just fine; that despite their destitution, they would find help to continue their journey to Kansas, their final destination. Many Exodusters viewed their journey as a divinely ordained mission of freedom. The biblical Exodus story spoke of a similar escape from oppression. As Eddie Glaude, Jr., notes, "the story's account of bondage, the trials of the wilderness, and the final

2. *St. Louis Globe-Democrat,* March 17, 1879.
3. Athearn, *In Search of Canaan,* 9.

entrance into the promised land resonated with those who experienced the hardships of slavery and racial discrimination."[4]

The penniless people who landed on the St. Louis levee that cold day were part of an unorganized movement that would bring as many as 20,000 Southern African Americans through St. Louis during 1879 and 1880.[5] Over one third of that number entered St. Louis during an intense period of migration in March and April of 1879. In February, the first migrants had caused hardly a ripple of excitement; by April 1, Exodusters landing in St. Louis was such a common occurrence that the *Globe-Democrat* featured a headline indicating no migrants had landed the day before.[6]

The flight of the Exodusters was also known nationwide and became an international story, as stories sympathetic to their plight appeared in the *Times* of London. In a front-page story on April 29, the *New York Times* estimated that 8,600 Exodusters had entered St. Louis in the previous two months; the paper also noted that there were more Exodusters arriving nearly every day. Only 2,400 of the 8,600 people who had landed on the St. Louis levee in March and April had been able to afford their own transportation to Kansas. The rest had been sent on with money raised by St. Louis's African American community, which housed, clothed, and fed the migrants in addition to finding transportation for them.[7]

This migration became known, somewhat mockingly, as the Kansas Fever Exodus because of its disorganized appearance and the naïveté of its participants. Many of the Exodusters believed that the federal government would supply them with free transportation from St. Louis to Kansas and, upon arrival in the Promised Land, forty acres of land for farming, as well as tools and other supplies until their land became productive. Unfortunately, their thoughts were wrong; there was going to

4. Voorhees Committee Report, pt. 2, 36–37; *St. Louis Globe-Democrat,* March 22, 1879; Painter, *Exodusters,* 190–95; Eddie S. Glaude, Jr., *Exodus! Religion, Race, and Nation in Early Nineteenth-Century Black America,* 3.

5. Cox Richardson, *The Death of Reconstruction,* 160; Voorhees Committee Report, pt. 2, 68, 254. The estimated numbers of Exodusters who passed through St. Louis vary somewhat, but are generally thought to have been between 10,000 and 20,000.

6. *St. Louis Globe-Democrat,* April 1, 1879.

7. *New York Times,* April 29, 1879.

be no government help. Any help the Exodusters received was going to have to come from other sources.[8]

Earlier in the decade most migrations of African Americans to Kansas and other western states had consisted of colonies of self-sufficient farmers who were somewhat similar in economic status to white homesteaders. These homesteaders usually worked collectively and were equipped with livestock, wagons, seed, implements, and everything necessary for the difficult task of building a life out of the soil of the plains. Some historians have labeled any African Americans who left the South for Kansas in the latter half of the nineteenth century as Exodusters. However, in 1879, the migration changed both in the quantity of migrants and in their condition. The Kansas Fever Exodusters bore little resemblance to the relatively well-equipped, well-organized earlier migrants; in outlook, planning (or lack thereof), and need they were different from other migrants. Most of the Exodusters were struggling economically in the South to begin with; paying four dollars' deck passage apiece for the eight-day steamboat trip from Vicksburg to St. Louis often completely depleted their already scant resources.[9]

Entering St. Louis possessing little more than the clothes on their backs and what goods they could carry, they resembled refugees from war more than homesteaders. Andrew Pollard, a former state senator from Mississippi who had joined the Exodus, later spoke to members of the St. Louis community and insisted that the Exodusters were not a colony and were not emigrants. They were instead, in his words, "refugees, fleeing from oppression and bondage."[10] As refugees, they were not expected to be as fully equipped as colonists. Instead, they resembled people who had packed up everything that they could carry and escaped. One observer, covering the Exodus for *Scribner's,* described their destitution: "Few of the immigrants had furniture, bedding, stoves, or dishes, and their wearing apparel was, as has been hinted, scant and threadbare; scores of the men were without coats or a change of shirts; most of the women had but one frock each and no wraps or stockings;

8. *St. Louis Globe-Democrat,* March 12, 1879.

9. Cohen, *At Freedom's Edge,* 175; Athearn, *In Search of Canaan,* 9.

10. *St. Louis Globe-Democrat,* March 18, 1879; other newspapers, including the *Kansas Pioneer* and the *New York Times,* also referred to the Exodusters as refugees.

half the children were barefoot and clad only in single cotton garments." Such conditions led to health problems; approximately six weeks into the Exodus a health report stated that dozens of Exodusters were suffering from bronchitis, malarial fever, diarrhea, pneumonia, dysentery, and measles. Lack of proper clothing, shelter, and nutrition caused Exodusters to die by the hundreds, leading to a mortality rate that one observer called "appalling."[11]

The Exodus was a movement of families, and sometimes the Exodusters arrived in family-sized groups. However, often there were dozens and even hundreds landing together on the St. Louis riverfront. In one instance, 200 travelers from a Baptist church in Delta, Louisiana, migrated together. Most Exodusters would camp along the banks of the Mississippi River, waiting to be picked up by the northern-moving riverboats. The *New York Times* reported on one group of Exodusters waiting for transportation on the riverbank north of Vicksburg. Unlike many Exodusters, they had money, but like most they were peaceable, cheerful, and anticipating success. Although they had been waiting "for some time," they were confident that a government-sponsored riverboat would provide their deliverance. Like others, these Exodusters would wait in vain for a government vessel; instead, they would have to rely on being picked up by private riverboats. Often, they waited in vain, as bulldozers would threaten the riverboat captains who picked up the refugees. One report stated that during the last week of April, nearly 2,000 Exodusters waiting on the riverbank watched riverboat after riverboat pass them by. The long wait caused many of them to suffer from exposure and also to use up their scant provisions. The same *Times* report noted that other groups waiting were not as fortunate as the group north of Vicksburg. The article reported, "At Bullitt's Bayou, 10 miles from Natchez, nearly 100 men, women, and children are begging passing steamers to take them. Some have money; others have none." Like others, the *Times* reporter noted the similarity between the Exodusters and refugees from war, writing, "at Natchez Under the Hill the scene reminds one of war times, when the fleeing negroes filled every town where Federal troops held possession." After finally

11. Henry King, "A Year of the Exodus in Kansas," 214; *St. Louis Globe-Democrat,* April 25, 1879; Guernsey, "The Negro Exodus," 374.

getting picked up and traveling upriver, the Exodusters entered the city of St. Louis.[12]

Sitting at the confluence of the Mississippi and Missouri rivers, St. Louis was "the pivot of the trip, the point where a trip northward became a trip westward." A simple riverboat ride on the Missouri River across the state to Wyandotte, Kansas, would complete the Exodusters' journey to a land that many considered a modern Canaan. Unfortunately, the majority of the Kansas Fever Exodusters landed in St. Louis without the ability to pay for the last leg of their trip. Destitute, with no visible means of support or aid, the Exodusters faced a choice. Would they continue their attempt to leave the South? Or would they turn back, accepting the riverboat companies' offers of free transportation back down the river? Ultimately, most decided to press on to Kansas. The story of their flight from racial, political, and economic oppression garnered attention and sympathy, and their journey became a political statement that was, at its core, about that most cherished of American values: freedom. As Reconstruction ended, the Exodusters were asserting a right that all Americans are supposed to enjoy—the right to pick up and start over, to begin again, to move to wherever opportunity is greatest for one's family. As violence and lack of opportunity pushed them out of the South, and the hope for a better life pulled them to Kansas, the Exodusters were, in essence, "pursuing happiness."[13]

Unfortunately for the Exodusters, acting on their right to move was a dangerous undertaking that would require help from numerous sources. The first of these sources, and perhaps the most important, was the African American community in St. Louis. Other groups that eventually aided the Exodusters were white Northern Republicans, former abolitionists, Quakers, and government officials from Kansas. However, it was the African American community in St. Louis that first stepped into the breach and led the efforts to help the Exodusters get through the city and continue journeying west. To the Exodusters waiting on the banks of the Mississippi for a riverboat, the Exodus felt like an escape, and most who reached St. Louis vowed never to return to the

12. *Christian Union,* September 10, 1879; Fletcher Report, 16–17; *New York Times,* May 22, 1879.

13. Glen Schwendemann, "Saint Louis and the 'Exodusters' of 1879," 36; Athearn, *In Search of Canaan,* 6–7.

South. Despite the hardships of their journey and the difficulties of the future, they still felt that leaving the South was their only option. When one Exoduster complained that he could not be in worse shape than by being stuck in St. Louis without any money, others in his party corrected him, asserting that being in the South was to be in the worst shape possible. The complaining Exoduster quickly agreed. But although being in St. Louis was considered an improvement, St. Louis was not the destination that the Exodusters sought.[14]

Nell Irvin Painter writes, "St. Louis occupied a pivotal position in the mythology of the Exodus. It linked the two parts of the idea, negative and positive, slavery and freedom." This pivotal position was not lost on the Exodusters, who understood that Missouri had been a slave state and that St. Louis, in many ways, represented the last obstacle to cross before finally escaping the South. In keeping with the biblical theme of the Exodus, one refugee told a St. Louis reporter, who quoted him in dialect, "Dis is our Red Sea, right hyah in St. Louis, atween home an' Kansas, an' if we sticks togeder an' keeps up our faith we'll git to Kansas an' be out o' bondage for shuah." In short, he was equating St. Louis with the barrier that Moses and the Israelites crossed on the way out of slavery.[15]

The people of the Exodus that others across the nation would later read about in the pages of newspapers and government reports were witnessed in person by Charlton Tandy as he watched the approximately 250 Exodusters milling around in the snow on the St. Louis riverfront the afternoon of March 12, 1879. Tandy noted the winter weather and the desperate condition of the men, women, and children on the levee, some of whom were wearing three or four pairs of pants to try to combat the cold. Tandy immediately began finding them housing for the night. He spent the rest of the day asking friends and acquaintances to take some Exodusters in while finding others positions with various businesses. For some, the best Tandy could do on such short notice was to find them shelter on wharf boats, which at least got them out of the freezing conditions. In securing a modicum of relief for the Exodusters, a local paper stated that Tandy had "succeeded remark-

14. *St. Louis Globe-Democrat,* March 12, 1879.

15. Painter, *Exodusters,* 195; *St. Louis Globe-Democrat,* March 19, 1879.

ably well and done himself great credit." Tandy would spend much of the next two years continuing and expanding the work he began on that cold afternoon.[16]

A respected, hard-working member of the St. Louis African American community, Charlton Tandy was a Civil War veteran, a well-known speaker, and a staunch Republican who worked as a messenger in the St. Louis customs house, a job that testified to his political connections. Tandy was born in Kentucky in 1836 to parents who were free only because his grandparents had purchased the family's freedom three years before his birth. Seventy-five years later he reiterated the value he placed on freedom by showing the yellowing freedom papers to a reporter as he talked about his family. Throughout his childhood, Tandy's family worked to free slaves through the Underground Railroad, and as a young man Tandy often led slaves on the route from Covington, Kentucky, to freedom in Cincinnati, Ohio.[17]

Tandy moved to St. Louis in 1857 in search of employment and to work on the Underground Railroad in Missouri. He worked a series of jobs until the Civil War began, then became post messenger at Jefferson Barracks. The war proved good for Tandy's standing, as he rose from state militia volunteer to captain of "Tandy's St. Louis Guard," an African American state militia that he recruited; he carried the honorific title of "Captain" for the rest of his life. With an appointment by the governor, Tandy and his militia were charged with helping to defend St. Louis in the event of a Confederate attack. His service earned him the notice of several political leaders, and after the war he even received recognition from President Ulysses S. Grant. Later in Tandy's life, after Theodore Roosevelt's decision to dine with Booker T. Washington caused a furor among segregationists, he noted, "But as for sitting at table with white men, I have had the pleasure of being there with the best

16. Tandy, in his testimony before the Voorhees Committee, is somewhat unclear when asked when the first Exodusters arrived in St. Louis. He correctly states that it was late February, but then gives the impression that his attention was called to the Exodus at that time. However, that is not the case. The February contingent of Exodusters made their own way into the city without any aid. Tandy finds out about the Exodus and begins organizing relief efforts when he meets the second boatload of Exodusters on March 12, 1879. *St. Louis Globe-Democrat,* March 13, 1879; Voorhees Committee Report, pt. 2, 37, 290.

17. Charlton H. Tandy Papers.

in the land. I once lunched with President Grant and in 1870 dined with Gov. Crittenden and Senator Cockerill [Cockrell] in Warrensburg."[18]

In the same year he claimed to have lunched with Ulysses S. Grant, Tandy contested St. Louis's growing Jim Crow segregation system by trying to stop the use of segregated streetcars. The story is descriptive of Tandy's method of personally fighting injustices. Three years earlier, in 1867, the president of the North Missouri Railroad had written to Missouri Republican leaders, asking them to desegregate the St. Louis public transportation system. African Americans were not allowed to stand or sit inside the cars; they were forced to either stand on the outside platform of the cars or walk. The president complained that even in the coldest weather, he had seen neatly dressed African American mothers holding their babies while riding on the outdoor platforms. With the vote for African American suffrage occurring the next year, the Missouri Republicans did not want to risk a fight over segregated streetcars, so they refused to pass legislation banning the system.[19]

In July 1867, Caroline Williams was pregnant and carrying a baby as she tried to board the Bellefontaine Railroad; the conductor pushed her away and would not let her board. Williams and her husband filed suit, and although no money was awarded, the streetcar lines were ordered to let African Americans ride inside the cars. Three years later, the court orders were still not being followed as African Americans in St. Louis were continually forced to ride on the platforms. Tandy finally decided to take matters into his own hands. He was not a large man, but he would grab the streetcar horses' reins and refuse to let them go until the conductors allowed the African Americans on board to ride inside the car. More often than not the conductors and other whites would fight with Tandy; he was once arrested on three consecutive days for his protests.[20]

Although Tandy was arrested, his political connections paid dividends as prominent businessmen and politicians paid his bail. Erastus Wells, the entrepreneur who had introduced the streetcar to St. Louis and was serving as a congressman from Missouri, appeared on Tandy's

18. John A. Wright, Sr., *No Crystal Stair: The Story of Thirteen Afro-Americans Who Once Called St. Louis Home,* 36; Charlton Tandy Papers.

19. Charlton Tandy Papers; Wright, *No Crystal Stair,* 38.

20. Wright, *No Crystal Stair,* 38; Nathan B. Young, *Your St. Louis and Mine,* 11.

behalf in court. Wells stated that Tandy was in the right and that his streetcar line would permit African Americans to sit anywhere that they wanted. Tandy led a boycott of the competing streetcar lines that refused to follow Wells's lead, and African Americans began to exclusively use Wells's integrated lines. The boycott worked and the rival companies began to change their policies, but the fight against discrimination on St. Louis streetcars was not over. In 1900, thirty years after his boycott and six years after he was admitted to the bar, Tandy sued the St. Louis Transit Company for $2,500 after a conductor caused his wife, Annie, to fall as she was exiting a segregated streetcar. The fall broke two of her ribs, gave her bruises, and impaired her hearing. The Tandys won the case, but were only awarded damages of $600. The suit was a continuation of Tandy's lifelong fight against racism.[21]

Tandy first gained notice statewide among Missouri Republicans in 1870 when he spent four months touring the state, speaking on behalf of the liberal wing of the Republican Party. Tandy was able to turn his connections into patronage jobs and a prominent place among Missouri's sizable African American Republican constituency. He held posts ranging from U.S. land agent and deputy U.S. marshal in New Mexico and Oklahoma to custodian of records at the St. Louis courthouse. Nine years later, Tandy tried to use his political connections to obtain relief for the Exodusters, but he found that most white political leaders in St. Louis were going to be of little help.[22]

The day after first helping the Exodusters find ad hoc shelter, Tandy received a letter from an acquaintance who had formerly been the secretary of the Mullanphy Board. The Mullanphy Board was a St. Louis charity founded nearly twenty years earlier when Bryan Mullanphy, son of a wealthy family, bequeathed half a million dollars to aid settlers who were stranded in St. Louis on their way west. Mullanphy, former circuit court judge and mayor of St. Louis, was a lifelong bachelor who had no children. In his will, he left two-thirds of his estate to his sisters and one-third "to the City of St. Louis, in the State of Missouri, in trust, to be and constitute a fund to furnish relief to all poor emigrants and travelers coming to St. Louis, on their way, bona fide to settle in the

21. Supreme Court of Missouri, case no. 10,746, October 1902, located in Charlton Tandy Papers.

22. *St. Louis Argus*, September 5, 1919.

West." Mullanphy's intention was that St. Louis would grow as a way station for travelers moving west, with his fund providing opportunity to those who would otherwise not have it.[23]

In the letter, Tandy's acquaintance told him that according to the will and the terms of the charity any bona fide emigrants, regardless of color, were entitled to some help from the board. Encouraged by this discovery, Tandy led a group of Exodusters to the Mullanphy Board offices to see the current secretary of the board, a Mr. Laveille, to ask for relief for the Exodusters. His request was quickly denied, as Laveille insisted that there were too many Exodusters to help and that the board's funds would soon be exhausted if they were offered aid. Tandy, who felt that "his people were not being given a fair show," persisted in asking for aid, but Laveille was dismissive, informing Tandy that he "did not wish to discuss the question."[24]

Charlton Tandy was not one to take such a brush-off lightly, especially when he felt that race was the reason behind the treatment. Instead of giving up, he and the Exodusters went to see Mr. Hill, the board president, to insist that the Exodusters be given a full hearing before the board. Hill did not believe that the Exodusters should receive relief from the board, but at Tandy's insistence he agreed to let him present his case to the entire board, which coincidentally was scheduled to meet later that afternoon. At the meeting, Tandy and the Exodusters he had brought with him crowded into the meeting room; they were forced to quietly wait for two hours while the board conducted its business. Because of the urgency of the situation, the pressing need for aid, and the presence of the Exodusters at the meeting, Tandy hoped that the board would address the Exoduster matter quickly. When that did not happen, he thought the board members would introduce the Exoduster question at the end of their regular meeting session. That did not happen either. Instead, Tandy was dismayed to learn that the board was going to adjourn without mentioning his request.[25]

Undeterred, Tandy called out to a Mr. Scruggs, a Democrat who served on the board, and asked to be allowed to address the group.

23. Morris Gluckin, "History of the Bryan Mullanphy Emigrant and Travelers Relief Fund," 1; Marshall D. Hier, "Judge Bryan Mullanphy, Brilliant, Benevolent, Bizarre."

24. Voorhees Committee Report, pt. 2, 37; *St. Louis Globe-Democrat,* March 13, 1879.

25. Vorhees Committee Report, pt. 2, 37.

When Scruggs was hesitant, Tandy stated that he only needed five minutes, and as Scruggs went back to address the other board members, Tandy continued to stare Scruggs in the eye. When Scruggs asked him why he was staring at him, Tandy replied, "I am reading the contour of the expression of your face; and I propose, sir, to direct my remarks directly to you, because I think I can approach you and get some help for these men that are in a suffering condition." Under Tandy's steady gaze, Scruggs relented, and recommended to the other members that Tandy be allowed to speak. Tandy spoke for a short time, describing the Exodusters' predicament and explaining why the board's help was vital to the group of stranded migrants.[26]

By the end of the meeting, the Mullanphy Board had pledged $100 to the Exodusters for immediate relief, giving the money to an Exoduster named Mr. Frederick. The board also appointed Reverend Lack, the superintendent of the St. Louis Provident Association, to dole out bread to the hungry migrants still on the levee. The board was not pleased with the Exodusters' request, and, after speaking with city officials, issued a resolution stating, "That information having come to this Board that the large body of applicants for transportation, now in this city, is but the forerunner of an exodus from the South. It is incompatible with the execution of the Mullanphy bequest to furnish transportation to any such body of persons, and that the President shall take notice of this." Eventually, after repeated requests from the St. Louis African American relief community, the board donated $450 to the Exodusters, but this money was given without dedicated support from St. Louis Mayor Henry Overstolz, who was an ex officio member of the board and controlled much of the board's spending. In his mayor's message, Overstolz made the argument that the Mullanphy fund did not apply to the Exodusters because the Exodusters were traveling in colonies, although this was not actually the case. He stated, "It may be stated that the funds of the bequest have never been expended in the transportation of colonies of people, either white or black, even where there is a definite location in view as an objective point."[27]

26. Ibid., 37.

27. *St. Louis Globe-Democrat,* March 14, 1879; Voorhees Committee Report, pt. 2, 37; *New York Times,* May 10, 1879; Gluckin, "History of the Bryan Mullanphy," 81–82.

In May, support from the Mullanphy Board dried up completely as Overstolz began to put conditions on the small amount of aid that the board was giving the Exodusters. With the African American community resources significantly depleted after carrying the burden of caring for thousands of refugees, a member of the St. Louis relief effort went to Overstolz one last time to ask for more help. Overstolz insisted on a public statement from the St. Louis African American community leaders discouraging the Exodus. After protesting the conditions, the St. Louis relief effort refused to ask the Mullanphy Board for any additional aid. In one of the earliest stories about the Exodus, the *Globe-Democrat* noted that "the Board recognizes its duty in treating Negroes the same as white people; but at the same time it does not like to shoulder the responsibility of sending out to Kansas colored people without any means to settle." To the African American community, the point was helping the Exodusters escape the South and get to Kansas; figuring out what to do next could come later.[28]

Bryan Mullanphy's original interest in helping travelers and migrants was kindled by a scene thirty years earlier that had been eerily similar to the Exodus. Despite the obvious resemblance, the similarities between the first group to receive Mullanphy's help and the Exodusters were either lost on the city officials, or they were deliberately ignored. In 1849, when Mullanphy was mayor, he had witnessed thousands of destitute Irish immigrants, many of them sick with typhus, stranded on the riverbanks of St. Louis after traveling by boat up the Mississippi River from New Orleans. Upon seeing these unfortunate people, Mullanphy ordered all cabs necessary to take the travelers to the City Hospital for treatment and ordered that all expenses be charged to the city of St. Louis. After this episode, Mullanphy regularly helped miners, artisans, farmers, and other travelers who arrived penniless in St. Louis.[29]

Building on this tradition of helping suffering, destitute travelers who were trying to get through the Gateway to the West, the Mullanphy Board had not required white settlers to have means before assisting them. Between 1868 and 1874, the board had assisted 10,373 settlers, even paying transportation costs to bring 8,856 people to Missouri from as far away as New York. Of these beneficiaries, many of whom were

28. *New York Times,* May 10, 1879; *St. Louis Globe-Democrat,* March 14, 1879.
29. Gluckin, "History of the Bryan Mullanphy," 9–10.

European immigrants, 7,721 were sent to the Mullanphy Emigrant Home on Fourteenth and Mullanphy streets. At the home, the immigrants were given room and board until they found employment and had the means to continue their journey or had their own place to stay in St. Louis. The home contained thirty to fifty settlers on average, and before closing in 1877 it had provided 24,446 days of room and board to people moving West. In its 1874 report, the Mullanphy Board reported assets of $700,000 and a rapidly increasing annual income of $30,000. In 1879, after a dispute that was unrelated to the Exodus, the city's attorney had concluded that poor travelers coming from any direction to settle in the West were included in the terms of Mullanphy's will. In spite of this decision, destitute African American travelers moving up through St. Louis to farms in Kansas were told that they did not qualify for assistance. To Tandy and the other members of the St. Louis African American community, a clear double standard was at work.[30]

Tandy was not happy with the amount of the initial Mullanphy Board donation, and vented his anger eight days later at a community meeting. At the meeting, Tandy "condemned in the harshest terms the action of the members of the Mullanphy Board," because of its small donation to the Exodusters. Tandy knew of cases where individual white families were given $300 to go west, yet hundreds of destitute African Americans were only given the equivalent of $100 collectively. He pointedly asked, "What kind of justice was this?" Given the number of Exodusters, the amount of money the Mullanphy Board controlled, and the relief that the board had offered to destitute migrants in the past, the $100 donated by the Mullanphy Board to the Exodusters was insulting to Tandy. However, the symbolism of how the donation was obtained is important. Charlton Tandy demanded that he be heard and that the Exodusters be treated as human beings. Tandy also showed that he was willing to confront the white power structure in St. Louis; in aiding the Exodusters, other St. Louis African American leaders would prove their willingness too.[31]

After helping the first group of Exodusters that he had encountered, and understanding that more Exodusters were reportedly on their way to

30. Florence Kidd, "Efforts to Encourage Immigration to Missouri after the Civil War," 51–56; Gluckin, "History of the Bryan Mullanphy," 84.

31. *St. Louis Globe-Democrat,* March 21, 1879.

St. Louis, Tandy realized that he could not organize the relief efforts on his own. Since his attempts at gaining aid through the white-controlled Mullanphy Board had been disappointing, he turned to the African American community for help. He knew that the community was willing to help; his friends and others in the community had been housing and feeding Exodusters since their arrival. The circular that Tandy distributed on March 14 shows that he viewed Exoduster relief as a collective responsibility of the African American community. He wrote, "We, the undersigned, realizing the immediate necessity of some actions being taken to make provision for the temporary relief of *our race,* known as emigrants, passing through our city on their way seeking homes in the Far West; and whereas, their destitute condition demands the attention of those who are in sympathy with suffering humanity, we do hereby call for a mass-meeting of *our citizens* (Italics mine)." The circular connects the Exodusters, the African American community, and citizenship, and reinforces the idea that the relief should be temporary, since the Exodusters' ultimate goal was to move beyond St. Louis.[32]

On March 16, less than a week after Tandy helped the 250 Exodusters, the Anchor Line steamer *Grand Tower* landed in St. Louis with a load of between 500 and 600 more Exodusters who were desperate for help. The landing made this group the third to arrive in St. Louis within three weeks, and increased the number of Exodusters in the city to between 700 and 800. The Exodusters who had the means to do so continued on to Kansas, but hundreds remained in St. Louis, needing assistance. Furthermore, the ship's captain reported that there were thousands of migrants waiting along the river for transportation to St. Louis. A local paper stated that it was apparent that the previous Exodusters were simply an advance guard of a much larger movement. In light of this information, it was imperative that the African American community meet to decide how best to proceed with their relief efforts.[33]

Plans for Tandy's meeting were organized through the African American churches; the meeting was to be held at St. Paul's Chapel on March 17. Organized in 1841, St. Paul's was the oldest African Methodist Epis-

32. Ibid., March 14, 1879.

33. *Missouri Republican,* March 17, 1879; *St. Louis Globe-Democrat,* March 17, 1879; *New York Times,* March 17, 1879.

copal church west of the Mississippi, and during the slavery era its congregation was a combination of both slaves and free African Americans. The brick structure its members built in 1871 was, for its time, one of the few churches in St. Louis built entirely by African Americans. The St. Paul's congregation of 1,200 people made it the largest African American Methodist church in the city.[34]

As would happen during the modern civil rights movement nearly one hundred years later, the African American churches became centers of organization, relief, and protest. St. Paul's, the Eighth Street Baptist Church, the Lower Baptist Church, and other churches provided space, money, volunteers, and, perhaps most importantly, encouragement to both the Exodusters and those helping them. The African American churches eventually played such a large role in the Exoduster relief effort that the *Globe-Democrat* referred to the Committee of Twenty-Five as the Immigrant Relief Committee of the Colored Churches. St. Paul's had been involved in litigation in the months leading up to the Exodus and was deeply in debt, owing $2,000 that was to be paid on a second deed. Although the money was due in June, the congregation spent most of its time, money, and energy in the spring of 1879 helping the Exodusters rather than concentrating on the church's financial difficulties. This dedication and concentration of resources reinforces the importance that the community placed on the Exodusters and their journey.[35]

Hundreds of people attended the organizational meeting, electing two secretaries, a treasurer, two vice presidents, and Tandy as president. In addition to these positions, they also elected a committee on resolutions that immediately went to work. The seven-person committee on resolutions included a veritable who's who of the St. Louis African American community. The resolutions committee named as its chair John Johnson, a well-respected customs house clerk and attorney. The committee also included John W. Wheeler, a tobacco contractor and one of only two African American at-large members elected to the city's

34. *New York Times,* March 17, 1879; N. Webster Moore, "The History of the St. Paul African Methodist Episcopal Church (A.M.E.) in St. Louis Missouri"; David Lossos, *Early St. Louis Area Places of Worship: Chapels, Churches, Missions, and Synagogues;* Young, *Your St. Louis and Mine,* 26.

35. Suzanna M. Grenz, "The Exodusters of 1879: St. Louis and Kansas City Responses," 57; *St. Louis Globe-Democrat,* April 26, 1879.

Republican Central Committee, and the Reverend Moses Dickson, minister of the African Methodist Episcopal Church, one of the founders of Lincoln University, and a Republican delegate to every state convention from 1864 to 1878.[36]

Echoing the Declaration of Independence, the resolution they drafted indicates that the committee believed the Exodusters were migrating to claim their rights as Americans, and that successful completion of their journey was an important step for all African Americans: "Whereas, in the exercise of their inalienable rights, some of our people are emigrating from their present homes, seeking new homes and protection in the far West, and whereas the matter is one of great importance and moment to us as a race, and whereas it requires time for the careful and correct consideration of these matters." The resolution also empowered a committee of fifteen to act on behalf of the Exodusters and collect donations for their relief. Like Tandy's circular, the resolution emphasizes the connection between the St. Louis African American community and the Exodusters. The assembly adopted the resolution and moved that it be sent to President Hayes. Johnson appointed a committee of fifteen men to organize the relief efforts, and the Committee of Fifteen then elected the Reverend John Turner of St. Paul's as chairman.[37]

The composition of the Committee of Fifteen (which soon became the Committee of Twenty-Five) shows how central African American churches were to the relief effort in St. Louis as nine ministers joined the committee. With African American churches playing a vital role in the lives of St. Louis African Americans, and by having African American ministers serving as community leaders, St. Louis showed that the gains its African American community had made were ahead of most Southern areas. Painter notes that in the South, "In stark contrast to the heavy preponderance of ministers among outstanding Black men by the end of the nineteenth century, the generation serving as guides in the interracial world of the late 1860s and very early 1870s had very few preachers." Painter, Lawrence Levine, and others explain that before the Civil War African American churches were marginalized by

36. Wright, *No Crystal Stair,* 16; Lawrence O. Christensen, "The Racial Views of John W. Wheeler," 536.

37. *St. Louis Globe-Democrat,* March 18, 21, 1879.

society, and thus spent years becoming established following the Civil War. In St. Louis, however, the churches were long established, and ministers like Moses Dickson had been community and political leaders for years. These churches would provide the community resources necessary to undertake a task as large as providing the Exodusters relief.[38]

The Reverend Moses Dickson was often Tandy's ally in many of his endeavors, such as the Exoduster relief, but Dickson also led his own organizations and was no shrinking violet in his own right. Dickson, like Tandy, was politically astute, an organizer who worked for African American rights in many areas. Dickson's best-known accomplishment was the founding of the International Order of Twelve, of Knights and Daughters of Tabor, an African American fraternal society that claimed nearly 100,000 members at the time of Dickson's death. Dickson also joined with James Milton Turner in 1865 to become two of the forces behind the Missouri Equal Rights League. Before the Civil War, Dickson was an Underground Railroad organizer and founded the Knights of Liberty, an organization dedicated to ending slavery.[39]

Born free in 1824 in Cincinnati, Dickson became a barber at the age of sixteen and spent three years traveling the South by steamboat in order to see slavery up close. In the *Manual of the International Order of Twelve, of Knights and Daughters of Tabor,* a history of his organization, Dickson writes in the third person about his experiences in the South and how those experiences shaped his life. He writes, "In these travels he saw slavery in all its horrors; he witnessed such scenes of monstrous cruelty as caused his African blood to boil with suppressed indignation at the sight of the outrageous suffering of his people. What he saw in these three years made a lasting impression on his heart, and he became a life-foe to the slave-owner, the slave-driver and the slave-trader." Dickson saw his Exoduster relief work to be a continuation of his abolitionism. The Exodusters were the same allies; the Southern planters, the same enemies.[40]

38. Ibid., March 18, 1879; Painter, *Exodusters,* 11–13; Lawrence W. Levine, *Black Culture and Black Consciousness: Afro American Folk Thought from Slavery to Freedom,* 3–55.

39. Gerald Early, ed., *"Ain't but a Place": An Anthology of African American Writings about St. Louis,* 282.

40. Ibid., 286.

After moving to St. Louis in 1846, Dickson called together twelve men he met during his travels in the South. At a house on the corner of Green (now Lucas Avenue) and Seventh streets, Dickson explained to the men his plan for creating an organization dedicated to freeing the slaves in the South. The men, who were from South Carolina, Mississippi, Alabama, Virginia, Louisiana, North Carolina, Georgia, and Tennessee, were to go back to their home states and recruit trustworthy men who were dedicated to fighting a war to free the slaves. After agreeing to the plan, the men all took an oath that said, "I can die, but I cannot reveal the name of any member until the slaves are free."[41]

Dickson remained in St. Louis, organizing the movement and working on the Underground Railroad while his disciples recruited followers for the uprising that was scheduled to take place in 1856. Referring to himself as "The Chief," Dickson writes of his and the Knights' roles in the Underground Railroad. "The Chief was convinced that the underground railroad could be so arranged that it could do better and safer work, and that the Knights of Liberty, through their perfect organization, could systemize the business. The Chief soon had perfected his plans so that the fugitive slaves could be taken from any part of the slave States, in families or individuals, and landed in Canada or the Northern, Eastern or Western States." Dickson claimed that in a ten-year span 70,000 slaves were carried to freedom on the route that he and the Knights of Liberty devised. It is an unverifiable number, and frankly one that seems highly exaggerated, much like Dickson's claim that by 1856 the Knights of Liberty consisted of more than 47,000 well-armed, well-trained men who were ready to begin a war to free the slaves.[42]

Dickson wrote that the Knights planned to converge on Atlanta in July of 1857, but that he recognized signs of an impending war and counseled his men to wait because the North would soon be fighting to end slavery. John Brown's unsuccessful raid of Harper's Ferry seemed to be further proof to Dickson that a war was inevitable, and that the Knights of Liberty's best policy was to wait and be of service to the Union Army. Again, Dickson's numbers, as well as his foresight to predict a war four years in the future, seem highly exaggerated. He writes, "When President Lincoln issued his Proclamation, calling for Colored volun-

41. Ibid., 286.
42. Ibid., 291–93.

teers, every Knight of Liberty was enrolled in the Union Army; 147,200 perfectly drilled, courageous men. They knew that Lincoln's Proclamation was not worth the paper it was written on, if the Confederates were victorious. Did the negro fight? Let the history of the Civil War speak the truth. They were Uncle Sam's desperate and reliable fighters." The possibility of Dickson controlling a private army of more than 100,000 men is unbelievable; Dickson was essentially claiming that he controlled 75 percent of African American soldiers who fought for the Union. Why, outside of ego, he felt the need to exaggerate the importance of his organization is unclear when his verifiable work was impressive enough.[43]

Dickson did fight in the war, surviving combat to return to St. Louis. Beyond Dickson's own writings, little is known about the Knights of Liberty. They were a secret society that kept few records, and Dickson's *Manual of the International Order of Twelve, of Knights and Daughters of Tabor,* was written in 1891, decades after the fact. Even if the numbers of slaves helped by Dickson on the Underground Railroad or the membership of the Knights of Liberty was exaggerated, the very existence of the organization and Dickson's involvement show his commitment to African American freedom and his potential as a leader.[44]

Moses Dickson's involvement in the Missouri Equal Rights League is much more easily verified. The Missouri Equal Rights League was born in the defeat of the African American suffrage provision of the Missouri Constitution of 1865. That year, ninety-four African American leaders from St. Louis had submitted to the Radical Republican leaders a petition asking for an African American suffrage inclusion into the new constitution. Fearful that an African American suffrage inclusion in the constitution would cause the constitution's defeat, the Radicals decided against honoring the petition; instead, they supported a constitution that gave African Americans all civil rights except suffrage and office holding.[45]

In response, several hundred African Americans gathered in St. Louis to create the Missouri Equal Rights League, which would work for

43. Ibid., 292; James M. McPherson, *The Negro's Civil War: How American Blacks Felt and Acted during the War for the Union,* xvii.

44. Early, ed., *Ain't but a Place,* 288; Wright, *No Crystal Stair,* 16.

45. William E. Parrish, *A History of Missouri: Volume III, 1860–1875,* 146–47.

African American suffrage and equality in Missouri. The league argued that suffrage was the key to protecting all other citizenship rights; without the power of the vote, every other right was in danger. At the inaugural meeting of the league, the speakers included twenty-six-year-old James Milton Turner, in what would be his first public role as a leader. Turner would later draw acclaim as he was appointed minister to Liberia. The speakers stated that African Americans had died defending the nation during the Civil War, and had earned full equality. They then elected a seven-person executive committee; Dickson was the most prominent member. The committee was charged with the tasks of planning mass meetings, procuring speakers to travel the state speaking about African American issues, and preparing an address that expressed the difficulties of life for African Americans in Missouri.[46]

The Equal Rights League released a document titled *Address to the Friends of Equal Rights* that outlined its purpose. Like the later Exoduster resolution, the *Address* built much of its argument from the Declaration of Independence and explained the plight of African Americans in relation to the early colonists. As Gary Kremer writes, "without the vote, black people were being forced to submit to taxation without representation and were having to obey laws that they had no voice in framing. . . . the committee warned that the question of what to do with black people in the immediate postwar period would become the greatest issue before the Republic." It is easy to understand why Dickson, who valued the right to vote so highly and understood its importance, would volunteer to work to aid the Exodusters, refugees from the South who were leaving in part because of denial of their rights as citizens.[47]

At the same time that Dickson and the other members of the committee on resolutions were drafting their initial resolution, the rest of the assembled people were listening to Exoduster representatives denounce their lives in the South and explain why they were moving to

46. Lawrence Oland Christensen, "Black St. Louis: A Study in Race Relations 1865–1916," 181; Gary R. Kremer, *James Milton Turner and the Promise of America,* 18–20; Eric Sandweiss, ed., *St. Louis in the Century of Henry Shaw: A View beyond the Garden Wall,* 19–20, 69; Lorenzo J. Greene, Gary R. Kremer, and Antonio F. Holland, *Missouri's Black Heritage,* 95.

47. Kremer, *James Milton Turner,* 21–22.

Kansas. Andrew Pollard, the former state senator from Louisiana, who had stated that the Exodusters were "not emigrants, but refugees, fleeing from oppression and bondage," was speaking. Pollard's tale was unique among the Exodusters in that he was not in St. Louis voluntarily. In Louisiana, Pollard had been using his two teams to haul the Exodusters' luggage to the *Grand Tower* when a band of armed white men cocked their guns and commanded him to board the boat with the others. They claimed that because Pollard was helping others to leave, he was the cause of the Exodus, and they thought it best to get rid of him to try to stop the migration. Although Pollard protested, they forced him on board, where he had to borrow cash to pay his fare. With his wife and children crying on the riverbank, Pollard was forced to leave his two teams, his horse and buggy, and all of his possessions and travel to St. Louis with the Exodusters. Other speakers complained of terrorism and bulldozing, sexual outrages of African American women, and killings of men, women, and children as white bulldozers attempted to stop the Exodus.[48]

At the conclusion of the Exodusters' speeches the assembly adopted a resolution forming the Committee of Fifteen, an executive committee for Exoduster relief. The assembly took up a collection, gaining fifty dollars with which to aid the Exodusters. In a move that is indicative of the African American community's desire to make relief for the Exodusters a community effort, the meeting also adopted a resolution requesting that all African American social societies in the city donate five dollars. In addition, a finance committee was appointed to receive all donations for the Exoduster relief. Perhaps the most telling part of the meeting, though, was when Charles Starkes, a member of the resolutions committee, made a speech that expressed the feeling that helping the Exodusters was nothing less than a duty for the assembled African Americans.[49]

In his speech, Starkes also was highly critical of St. Louis Mayor Henry Overstolz, handling him, in the words of the local paper, "without gloves." Starkes criticized Overstolz because the mayor had decided that the Exodus should not continue and had begun searching for ways to try to stop it. On March 15, Overstolz sent a telegram to numerous

48. *St. Louis Globe-Democrat,* March 18, 21, 1879.
49. Ibid., March 18, 1879.

cities downriver in hopes of heading off further migration. The telegram stated, "it is my duty to warn the colored people against coming to this city without money to support themselves and to pay their way West. The City of St. Louis is wholly unable to support them or to furnish them means of reaching their destination. There are no opportunities of obtaining employment here at present, much suffering and destitution must certainly be endured by colored people coming to this city without money or friends." Fortunately for the Exodusters, although they did not have money, in St. Louis they had friends. And the St. Louis African American community was incensed that Overstolz was trying to persuade the Exodusters not to leave the South when their lives and livelihoods were in danger if they stayed.[50]

Since many Exodusters could not read and would not see the mayor's proclamation anyway, Overstolz's telegram was futile. In addition, mere words were not going to convince the Exodusters to return. As the *New York Times* wrote, "It does not seem to affect the volume of this emigration to warn the fugitives of the rashness of their venture. They are going, and they absolutely refuse to return." However, the proclamation would put the city of St. Louis as officially in opposition to the Exodus, an important position since its trading partners, the Southern planters, were gravely concerned about losing their labor force. The *Times* stated, "Here in St. Louis the mercantile class, commission merchants, and cotton brokers, all, in fact, who deal with the cotton and sugar section, desire to prevent the exodus. Public feeling among the well-to-do discourages its continuance." St. Louis business leaders needed cheap African American labor in the South to continue to produce a cotton crop to be shipped through the St. Louis market.[51]

The St. Louis business community had strong ties to the Southern planters, and the mayor knew that any threat to the Southern labor situation was potentially damaging to St. Louis business. Overstolz's understanding of the St. Louis business climate was formidable. He was a German immigrant who had moved to St. Louis as a young man and made fortunes in banking, insurance, and as a wholesale grocer. Successful enough that he was able to twice retire from business, Overstolz became involved in city politics and was elected to the city council in

50. Ibid., March 16, 18, 1879.

51. *New York Times,* April 7, May 10, 1879; *St. Louis Globe-Democrat,* April 21, 1879.

1849, becoming St. Louis's first native German to be elected to citywide office. He ran for mayor in 1875, but was defeated by James Britton in a narrow and controversial contest. Overstolz claimed it was a fraudulent election, and was vindicated nine months later as evidence of ballot-box stuffing and voter fraud became publicized. The city council ruled Overstolz the winner and he completed the remaining time of the two-year term. He was then elected to a four-year term in 1877, only a few months before a citywide labor strike. During the strike, Overstolz had been strongly criticized for his handling of the situation, for being indecisive and allowing the strikers to take control of the city. He had finally found some redemption in personally directing the charge that ended the strike and resulted in the arrests of its leaders. In hindsight, his reluctance to act hastily early in the strike may have prevented a bloody confrontation from occurring when emotions were highest. But the criticism still stung. The Exodus presented Overstolz with another crisis that, to his mind, also threatened the well-being of his city, albeit in a much different way.[52]

The proclamation that Overstolz released on March 15 was not the mayor's first effort in stopping the Exodus. Two days before, when, according to the local paper, he was "much at sea" over the crisis, he contemplated using a legal maneuver to block the arrival of Exodusters. In a reflection of the attitudes of the day, St. Louis had a city ordinance that prohibited the bringing of paupers into the city; steamboat companies or railroad lines that violated the ordinance could be subject to fines of $25 to $300 and be required to post a $1,000 bond to support the paupers. Overstolz made it clear that he intended to enforce the ordinance and fine the steamboat lines to convince them to stop carrying the Exodusters, but questions as to the legality of the ordinance were raised. The steamboat lines were common carriers and were thus subject to the Civil Rights Act of 1875, which stated that passengers could only be refused space on a common carrier if they lacked the proper fare. The Exodusters were able to pay their fare to St. Louis. The riverboat lines, which in many cases were refusing to pick up Exodusters in the South, were not encouraging the Exodus in any way. However, because

52. James Neal Primm, *Lion of the Valley: St. Louis, Missouri, 1764–1980,* 300–301; David T. Burbank, *Reign of the Rabble: The St. Louis General Strike of 1877,* 102–41; David Thelen, *Paths of Resistance: Tradition and Dignity in Industrializing Missouri,* 83.

they were picking up the Exodusters as paying passengers, they were being accused by the St. Louis leaders and Southern planters of encouraging and even causing the Exodus. Captain George Lennox of the *Grand Tower* denied that the Anchor Line Steamboat Company had any connection with convincing the Exodusters to leave the South. He stated that the Exodusters had paid their fare in advance; thus, passage was provided to them under the terms of the act. The Anchor Line came under special scrutiny from St. Louis city officials because it provided transportation to many of the Exodusters.[53]

Overstolz considered another tactic after legal solutions proved unwieldy. When word of the impending *Grand Tower* landing first reached St. Louis, Overstolz met with members of the Board of Health to determine if the Exodusters could be stopped at the St. Louis Quarantine Hospital, located twelve miles downriver from the city. The threat of yellow fever was on everyone's minds and St. Louisans were uneasy about the possibility of an outbreak. In 1878 and 1879, shortly before the Exodus, yellow fever became a major concern as epidemics struck many areas in the Mississippi River Valley; the 1878 epidemic was particularly destructive, killing at least 18,000 people from New Orleans to Tennessee. Memphis was hit especially hard as at least 5,000 of its 50,000 residents died from the disease and the majority of its citizens evacuated the city. These outbreaks received tremendous amounts of publicity in the St. Louis newspapers, especially after the disease spread to St. Louis for the first time in the city's history, although the spread was unrelated to the Exodus. The fear caused by yellow fever became an important issue to St. Louis as city officials considered using the epidemic as an excuse to distance themselves and the city from the Exoduster migration.[54]

St. Louis citizens were so worried about the disease that on March 10 a letter from the president of the Board of Health appeared in the paper to calm everyone's fears. The letter stated that yellow fever was not a problem downriver, and Memphis's last reported case of the disease had been in December. Still, many people believed that the destitute migrants might be carriers of the disease. During the Board of Health

53. *St. Louis Globe-Democrat,* March 14, 17, June 28, 1879; Painter, *Exodusters,* 232.

54. *Missouri Republican,* March 16, 1879; Khaled J. Bloom, *The Mississippi Valley's Great Yellow Fever Epidemic of 1878,* 1, 280–81.

meeting, it was finally determined that expense outweighed concerns over the city's health. If the Exodusters were put into quarantine and comfortably cared for, Overstolz felt there was no guarantee that they would ever leave the city. Overstolz and the Board of Health decided instead that the migrants should be allowed to enter St. Louis—hopefully to leave as soon as possible without posing too much danger to its citizens.[55]

Nearly every boat that landed in March and April carried Exodusters. As more refugees landed in St. Louis, Overstolz and the city's officials washed their hands of any responsibility, limiting their response to providing some basic health care and policemen for protection against criminals at the wharf. The policemen were necessary as St. Louis's criminal element began preying on the migrants. Although, as one newspaper pointed out, "the baggage was generally of such a character as to offer few temptations to thieves," there were pimps and confidence men who tried to take advantage of the Exodusters. The policemen on the wharf also read Overstolz's statement to the new arrivals. However, any attempt to dissuade the Exodusters was unsuccessful; the paper reported that they were "exceedingly suspicious of white men . . . and are inclined to distrust all statements which tend to discourage them in the expectation of perfect bliss at the end of their journey." This suspicion was no doubt partially due to the Exodusters' experiences in the South, but was also due to advice from the St. Louis African American community.[56]

The feelings of the white community about this advice can be seen in the reporting of the St. Louis newspapers. The *Missouri Republican* was actually a Democratic newspaper, and every edition stated that it was "dedicated to the interests of the West and of the South." It was not sympathetic to the Exodusters, and the Exodus received much less coverage in the *Republican* than it did in the Republican paper, the *Globe-Democrat.* However, the *Republican* provides important evidence about the St. Louis African American community's view of the Exodus. One *Republican* story indicated, "The colored population of the town manifested a lively interest in the welfare of their Southern brethren and some of them did much to keep up the spirits of the emigrants by

55. *St. Louis Globe-Democrat,* March 10, 16, 1879.
56. *Missouri Republican,* March 17, 1879; *St. Louis Globe-Democrat,* March 17, 1879.

telling them not to believe anything the white people told them, but to just go ahead to their journey's end and see for themselves as much as they liked." Two days later, the paper appeared to be insulted as it reported, "they pay no heed to anything a white man says, and evidently believe that they will do a great deal better to follow their own impulses than to be guided by advice coming from any not their own color."[57]

The Exodusters, however, were listening to the St. Louis African American community, and the community's encouragement was important to the Exodus. In a story in the *Globe-Democrat,* a reporter declares, "Several negroes who live in St. Louis were among the emigrants encouraging them to go ahead and never think of turning back." Later in the story, two of the few Exodusters who decided to leave Kansas and return to the South were interviewed. Neither man was able to find work in Kansas, and both had suffered deaths of family members during the journey. As they were being interviewed, a member of the St. Louis relief effort appeared and attempted to convince the Exodusters against returning to the South. The story says:

> It is also curious to note the stand taken by the local negro residents here who come in contact with the refugees.
>
> Anybody can satisfy himself any day by a trip to the levee that as soon as a boat arrives there are parties here who go among the deck passengers and use every effort to urge the emigrants to continue on their journey, notwithstanding the pitiful experience of a great number of those who have already gone forward. And whenever a little batch of worn, anxious wayfarers reach this city on their way back to the home of their birth, these same industrious busybodies are to be found circulating among them and filling their ears with the most absurd stories imaginable, all designed to deter them from going back to the South. These men will try to persuade them to leave the boats and try their luck in St. Louis or in Illinois, well knowing that this would only be to invite further hardship.[58]

The *Republican* and *Globe-Democrat* reporters were not the only people who believed that African Americans in St. Louis were encour-

57. *Missouri Republican,* March 17, 19, 1879.
58. *St. Louis Globe-Democrat,* May 16, 1879.

aging the Exodusters to continue. In a March 23 interview, Mayor Overstolz stated, "There are several agitators going about among the unfortunate creatures, urging them not to return south, but to remain here, penniless and without prospect of betterment, that they may assert their freedom of action." Everyone else failed to see the Exodusters as independent actors; instead, they debated over the causes of the Exodus and what to do with the Exodusters.[59]

The Southern planters and St. Louis business leaders wanted to halt the Exodus and send the Exodusters back down South; many politicians questioned the motives behind the Exodus. The *Nation,* in trying to be sympathetic, wrote, "the condition of the poor people . . . calls, of course for pity and charity. But the best friends of the negro cannot wish to encourage or to make themselves responsible for the further spread of the movement." In contrast, the St. Louis African American community, who knew the Exodusters needed their assistance, spoke with them and decided to do everything in their power to help them get to their destination. The St. Louis African American community wanted to open up as many options for the Exodusters as possible as a way to encourage them to leave the hardships of the South.[60]

It was going to take more than words and encouragement to help the Exodusters, though, and the African American community knew it. From March 17 through March 24, more than 2,500 Exodusters passed through St. Louis, with at least 2,000 being housed for several days by the African American community. On the evening of March 18, the steamer *John B. Maude* landed with between 200 and 300 Exodusters from Mississippi, fewer than 60 of whom were "able-bodied field hands." St. Louis police officers spent the evening in a partially successful attempt to stop a large group of Almond Street pimps from getting on board to entice the female Exodusters, although some of the women took them up on their offer.[61]

The next morning, members of the St. Louis relief group showed up to offer the Exodusters food and shelter at the local churches. On March 21, in a story headlined "Our Colored Visitors," the *Globe-Democrat*

59. Ibid., March 23, 1879.

60. *Nation,* April 10, 1879.

61. *Kansas Pioneer,* April 12, 1879; *Missouri Republican,* March 20, 1879; *St. Louis Globe-Democrat,* March 19, 1879.

reported that 1,400 Exodusters had arrived in St. Louis, and of those, 400 had continued on to Kansas. Of the thousand Exodusters who were still in St. Louis, only ten per day were able to find employment. The rest would be completely dependent on the relief provided by St. Louisans. For example, George Halliday arrived on the packet boat *Hard Times* with a group of twenty Exodusters, including several children. Halliday explained how the St. Louisans provided food and shelter for the Exodusters and booked their passage to Kansas on the *Fannie Lewis.* The relief workers even provided a doctor to care for Halliday's wife, who was ill from "misery in the left side." For the five days that they were in St. Louis, the men in Halliday's group searched for work as a way to earn money of their own, and although they were unsuccessful in finding employment, at least their immediate needs were taken of.[62]

To provide shelter for the Exodusters, the relief workers called on their connections in the local community. The Eighth Street Baptist Church and Lower Baptist Church were housing approximately 250 Exodusters apiece, and St. Paul's Chapel was caring for 150. The accommodations were austere at best, as there was never enough food and most Exodusters slept on the floor, huddled together among their belongings. St. Paul's lodged the Exodusters in a room off the main sanctuary, and the Exodusters chatted quietly among themselves as the services continued next door. The Eighth Street Baptist Church turned over its entire basement to such a large number of people that their laughter could be heard a block away. All three churches had guards posted at the entrances to keep out the criminals and the curious.[63]

Some Exodusters were not as fortunate and did not find shelter in the relatively safe churches. The remaining Exodusters were placed around town with various families, or took up residence in abandoned buildings. Happy Hollow, an African American tenement section, had tenements that contained as many as a dozen Exodusters in one room, and there were other reports of twenty-one Exodusters living in a two-room alley apartment. A report also stated twenty-five to thirty Exodusters had taken refuge in an abandoned house in St. Louis's western suburbs.[64]

62. Fletcher Report, 10–17.

63. *St. Louis Globe-Democrat,* March 21, 1879; *Missouri Republican,* March 20, 1879.

64. *Missouri Republican,* March 15, 19, 1879; *St. Louis Globe-Democrat,* March 23, 1879.

In a report given six weeks after the start of the Exodus, Dr. Joseph Moore of the St. Louis Board of Health described the living conditions of the Exodusters. The *Globe-Democrat* quoted him as saying, "all were living in the most uncomfortable and unhealthy quarters—families of from 6 to 10 persons cooking, eating, and sleeping on the floor, in the same room. They had no furniture of any kind—no bedsteads, no cook-stoves; and the food they toasted over a coal-fire in the hearth was scant—consisting of but corn bread and pork, and but poorly cooked." On April 4, two doctors reported 200 of the 500 Exodusters in St. Louis "are prostrated with malarial fevers and chills," and that the African American community was going to attempt to distribute the Exodusters throughout a wider area of the city. The Board of Health reported the Exodusters had illnesses that were worsening. The Exodusters, like other visitors to the city, complained about the nearly undrinkable, dirt-filled St. Louis water. It was a vulnerable time for the Exodusters, as they waited for days and even weeks on end, hoping that somehow they would make it through St. Louis.[65]

In one appalling incident, a member of the St. Louis African American community abused the trust and vulnerability of the Exodusters. Sylvia Ann Craxton was an eleven-year-old Exoduster who arrived with her parents on March 29. Her parents were given lodging in one of the crowded churches, while Sylvia Ann was placed in the care of Henry Alonzo Green, a man unknown to many in the tight-knit community, but who had been at the church for most of the day helping the Exodusters. Since it was common for members of the community to open up their houses to the migrants, Sylvia Ann's parents consented when Green said that she could spend the night with his children at his home in the western part of the city. Green promised to send her back to the church the next morning with a basket of provisions. As they walked to his house, Green stopped Sylvia Ann at Vandeventer Avenue, threw her to the ground, and sexually assaulted her before running away. Sylvia Ann was found wandering the streets by police, who eventually arrested and charged Green.[66]

65. *St. Louis Globe-Democrat,* April 4, 9, 25, 1879.

66. The local newspapers are inconsistent when giving Sylvia Ann's age and even her name. In the initial news stories of the incident, her name is given as Sylvina Croxton, and her age is said to be fifteen. On the eve of Green's trial, her name is given as Sylvania Ann

J. L. D. Ferrier, a well-known African American attorney, defended Green. Ferrier, who was a graduate of Oxford University and Cambridge and Massachusetts Law School, was described as being "one of the best educated and most highly cultured lawyers at the bar in St. Louis." Although Ferrier was highly praised for his "extensive knowledge of the law and great tact and ingenuity" during the trial, his task was a difficult one. Before the trial began, the *Globe-Democrat* described his client as "a brutal-looking mulatto . . . whose face alone will go far toward convicting him." The trial was held on May 6; Sylvia Ann and her parents had remained in St. Louis to testify to the attack. The *Globe-Democrat* offered this insensitive description of the victim, who had to be traumatized by her ordeal, but who had dressed in her finest clothes for her court appearance: "Her personal appearance was not such as to attract a great deal of sympathy. About eleven years of age, with a green ribbon about her wooly head on which was pitched a dilapidated felt hat, she wore a bright yellow skirt, a calico waist of several colors, a neck ornament consisting of a pink and a blue ribbon twisted together, and a red shawl. All this was set off against an ebony complexion, powdered with St. Louis limestone." In spite of her fear at the strange procedures (she did not know what it meant to take an oath or to understand the concept of perjury), the child bravely identified her attacker in a steady, but low voice. Others, including Sylvia Ann's father, identified Green and stated they had seen him leave the church with Sylvia Ann. Regardless of any problems with Sylvia Ann's testimony, the jury took only minutes to convict Green and sentence him to twenty years in the state penitentiary.[67]

Fortunately, Sylvia Ann Craxton's story was an extreme and very rare example of Exoduster mistreatment by the St. Louis African American community. Most Exodusters were supplied clothes, food, lodging, and transportation costs by the St. Louis African American community, who, it is important to note, were often economically little better off than

---

Claxton, and her age is given as ten. In the news story after the trial, her name is given as Sylvia Ann Craxton, and her age is said to be eleven. I have chosen to use the information from the final news story because the reporter was present in the courtroom, and he would have heard Sylvia Ann state her correct name and age during her testimony. *St. Louis Globe-Democrat,* May 6, 1879.

67. Ibid., April 1, May 6, 7, 1879; *Missouri Republican,* April 1, 1879.

the people they were helping. On March 20, with relief funds dwindling, a thousand Exodusters still in need of assistance, and at least another thousand on the way, the African American community held their second mass meeting, this time at a Washington Avenue church. This crowded meeting would prove to be much more contentious than the previous meeting, as a split appeared in the African American community between conservative and activist factions. The split would eventually grow wider, damage the credibility of the relief organizers, and hurt the relief effort.[68]

68. *Vicksburg Herald,* quoted in the *St. Louis Globe-Democrat,* March 20, 21, 1879. The *Globe-Democrat* states that it was the Wesley Methodist Church that hosted the meeting, while the *Missouri Republican* states that it was at a Baptist church, but both place the meeting at a church on Washington Avenue.

3

Encouraging the Exodus

I would never go South again; I never intend to go there again; I had enough money to get here with, but have not money to get to Kansas with.
— JAMES BROWN, EXODUSTER

The second mass meeting of the St. Louis African American community began with Charlton Tandy's aforementioned indignant speech against the Mullanphy Board, as well as with additional comments in which he stated that the reputation of the American people had been damaged by the outrages committed by Southern whites. Tandy's anger reflected the tension and frustration that was present during the meeting. The audience, composed mostly of African Americans but also containing a few supportive whites, was restless throughout the night, at one point singing a rousing rendition of "Hang Jeff Davis on a Sour Apple Tree." The Reverend John Turner issued a report stating that the Committee of Fifteen was too busy organizing the relief efforts to submit a written report, and he indicated that the size of the task had necessitated increasing the number on the committee from fifteen to twenty-five. In addition, Turner reported that subcommittees of finance, resolutions, transportation, reception, and entertainment should also be appointed. It was at this point that the meeting took an ugly turn.[1]

1. *Missouri Republican,* March 21, 1879; *St. Louis Globe-Democrat,* March 21, 1879.

Alfred Carter, who was not a member of the resolutions committee, took the floor and read a series of resolutions that placed the blame for the Exodus at the feet of the white South. Carter explicitly stated that abuse and mistreatment of African Americans in the South were the cause of the Exodus. He then proposed that there be an appointment of a standing committee, whose duty it would be to "encourage emigration from those Southern states from which these people come; to distribute circulars among them, and if need be go down in person and urge them to quit the land of oppression to move to a more genial clime." The debate that ensued over the proposal reinforces the argument that the St. Louis relief community viewed their role as more than relief and charity; they were actually encouraging the Exodus rather than just supplying charity for the Exodusters. Carter, with the support of Tandy, spoke at such length and with such venom that even his supporters finally called for him to take his seat. James Milton Turner, the former minister to Liberia, was the first to criticize Carter's speech, and Turner and Carter exchanged personal insults.[2]

It was not the first time that Turner found himself at odds with other African American leaders in St. Louis. He and Tandy had been both allies and rivals for years. Nine years earlier, as Tandy was gaining a reputation in Republican politics, he and Turner had found themselves on opposite sides of an issue, and their dispute turned personal. In 1870, the Radical Republicans and the Liberal Republicans were split over three amendments to the Missouri constitution and the upcoming gubernatorial election between the Liberal B. Gratz Brown and the Radical Joseph McClurg. McClurg had been elected governor in 1868, but an African American suffrage provision had been defeated as many whites refused to vote for African American suffrage until white rebels were enfranchised. Missouri was not alone, as the previous year Ohio, Kansas, and Minnesota had also rejected African American suffrage amendments.[3]

Later that year, after the ratification of the Fifteenth Amendment to the U.S. Constitution guaranteed African American men the right to vote, the Liberal Republicans were willing to enfranchise former rebels in Missouri, in hopes that there would be future concessions for

2. *Missouri Republican,* March 21, 1879.
3. Christensen, "Black St. Louis," 185.

African Americans. The three disputed amendments in the 1870 election promised to make it easier for rebels to be enfranchised, and promised to remove race as a barrier to public office. The Radical Republicans wanted to continue to punish the former rebels and thus were in opposition to the amendments.[4]

In hopes of drumming up African American support against the amendments, the Radicals called upon Turner, who had become well known in Missouri as an educator and leader of the Missouri Equal Rights League and who had great oratorical skill. Turner traveled the state speaking against the amendments, gaining support and building his reputation. However, his speeches were also polarizing, as many African Americans felt that his stand against the amendment jeopardized future cooperation and concessions for African Americans in Missouri. To counteract Turner, the Liberals called upon Tandy and another St. Louis African American leader, George Wedley. Wedley and Tandy traveled the state giving speeches in an attempt to draw African Americans to the Liberal side of the dispute. The opposition between the men was brutal, and often turned personal. Eventually, the Liberals were successful as the Radicals realized the tenuousness of their position and reversed course immediately before the election. A majority of African Americans supported the Radicals, but a coalition of Liberal Republicans and Democrats joined to elect Brown as governor.[5]

This defeat marked the end of Radical rule in Missouri, and once a Democrat replaced Brown in 1872, the Republicans would be shut out of the governor's mansion for the next thirty-seven years. Even in defeat, Turner was able to benefit from the reputation he had built and secured his post as minister to Liberia from President Grant, but it is likely that the bitterness of the competition between the Liberals and the Radicals remained an undercurrent in Turner's relationships with Tandy and Wedley. This bitterness can best be seen in 1872, when Turner arrived in St. Louis on a visit from his Liberian post. Reverend John Turner, Wedley, Moses Dickson, Tandy, and others greeted Turner at the train station in celebration of his return. Turner had somewhat of a love-hate relationship with other St. Louis African American leaders, many of whom thought him too pompous and self-serving. In spite of

4. Kremer, *James Milton Turner,* 40–51.

5. Ibid., 46–47; Greene, Kremer, and Holland, *Missouri's Black Heritage,* 105.

their differences, Turner's success was still cause for celebration in the African American community. Turner's decision to announce his intention to run for the Missouri House of Representatives, however, was too much for Wedley and he denounced Turner's decision. Later, at a reception for Turner, Turner insulted Wedley in very harsh terms. The next day on the street the two men had words, and although Turner walked with a permanent limp caused by a wound he received during the battle of Shiloh, he knocked Wedley down three times. Wedley in response pulled out his penknife and stabbed Turner in the left lung, severely wounding him and incapacitating him for months. Tandy and Turner also had a physical encounter. During the debates over the 1870 election, Turner bit Tandy on the hand as the two argued about the adoption of the disputed amendments. Given the history of animosity between the parties, it was almost guaranteed that James Milton Turner's involvement in the Exoduster relief would turn contentious.[6]

Tandy and Turner, who had first met in 1857 when Tandy arrived in St. Louis, never had another physical confrontation after the biting incident, but their relationship contained a great deal of distrust. This distrust helps to explain the conflicts that would arise between the two during the Exoduster relief. Turner thought Tandy small-time and out of his league as both an orator and leader, and Tandy felt that Turner was a self-promoter who would not get his hands dirty when it came to actually working for the betterment of average African Americans. Tandy was often more interested in local problems, while Turner had aspirations on a national scale. These contrasting goals led the two men to see the solutions to African American problems from different perspectives. They would work together when necessary, but oftentimes they were more rivals than allies, and Turner's mistrust and condescension of Tandy began to show itself during the Exoduster crisis.[7]

After Turner's criticism of Carter during the Exoduster relief meeting, John Wheeler, the future editor of the African American newspaper the *Palladium* and like James Milton Turner an iconoclast, asked to be recognized. Wheeler was a freeborn Kentucky native who worked as a servant in the Union Army during the Civil War. After the war, Wheeler lived in Indianapolis for a short time before moving to St. Louis in 1867.

6. Parrish, *A History of Missouri,* 149; Kremer, *James Milton Turner,* 47, 103–4.
7. Nieman, ed., *African Americans and the Emergence of Segregation,* 364.

Only twenty years old when he arrived in St. Louis, Wheeler found work in one of the city's many tobacco warehouses. It was a good career choice, as he spent his twenties moving steadily up the career ladder, rising from clerk to foreman. By the time he was in his early thirties, Wheeler was a tobacco contractor who employed as many as thirty men. As his professional career grew, so did Wheeler's involvement in public life and politics. He became very involved in Republican politics in 1872, and in 1879 was elected as an at-large member of the Republican City Central Committee for St. Louis.[8]

A Republican throughout his life, Wheeler was also a recipient of Republican patronage, accepting appointments given to him by Republican politicians. However, he never confined his activism to politics; racial issues also continually drew his attention, and the two issues were often entangled. From the early 1870s through the turn of the century, Wheeler was involved in nearly every affair that concerned St. Louis African Americans. From 1897 to 1911, his instrument to express his views on race, politics, and morals was the *St. Louis Palladium,* the weekly newspaper that he edited. Calling himself the "Palladium Man," Wheeler wrote that the newspaper was "An Afro-American Newspaper, Published for the Good of the Race." Lawrence Christensen argues that Wheeler often held conservative views and, like Booker T. Washington, "expressed the racial philosophy which he felt accounted for his own success." This racial philosophy held that African Americans should accumulate wealth and stand together by supporting African American businesses, should raise their moral standards, should work with their white allies to gain positions of power, and should not agitate the race question because agitation might make things worse.[9]

During the meeting, Wheeler objected that Carter was forcing himself upon the meeting, and that his resolutions were too strongly worded. Calling the resolutions "revolutionary and rebellious," Wheeler stated that if they were passed, they would place the St. Louis African American community against the entire South and against the white population, a position that could not be taken in times of racial turmoil. Wheeler insisted that he was not an enemy to whites and indeed looked upon whites as friends to him and his race. Furthermore, Wheeler intended to ask whites for help with the Exoduster relief. Any attempt

8. Christensen, "The Racial Views of John W. Wheeler," 536.

9. Ibid., 535–41, 547; *St. Louis Palladium,* November 11, 1905.

to declare hostility toward the white community would, in Wheeler's opinion, bring about disastrous results. He urged those present at the meeting to dismiss Carter's resolutions.[10]

After Wheeler's speech, the meeting quickly got out of hand. There was mass confusion that threatened to become a free-for-all as men were shouting and threatening one another. The split over the resolutions reflected the split in the African American community between the conservatives, who were seeking ways to work within the system to affect change peacefully, and the activists, who were demanding recognition of their equal rights immediately. Finally, two African American women in the audience, Mrs. Lizzie Haydock and Mrs. J. C. Mann, raised their hands and quieted the men. One of the women reminded the men that they were engaged in noble work and it was pathetic for them to be acting in such a disgraceful manner. Instead of meeting for displays of debate or displays of eloquence, she told them that they should remember they were assembled to devise ways to assist people who desperately needed help. In short, she scolded them and told them to get back to business. Chastised, the men did just that.[11]

Carter withdrew his resolutions, and John H. Johnson of the Resolution Committee put forth an alternative that the meeting adopted. The new resolution, while still calling for the removal of African Americans from the South, took on a milder tone than Carter's proposals. However, it still outlined the reasons the Exodusters were leaving the South and stated that they were within their rights to do so. The resolution also shows that the African American community in St. Louis recognized that the relief they were providing was serving a larger purpose than simple charity. In part, the resolution read:

> While in the exercise of their rights as citizens, and occupying the relation of tillers of the soil to the owners thereof, the owners of the land differing with them on the questions of politics, adopted

10. *Missouri Republican,* March 21, 1879; *St. Louis Globe- Democrat,* March 21, 1879.

11. The *Globe-Democrat* of the same day states that it was "one of the white ladies in the audience" who restored calm. I have chosen to use the *Republican*'s statement that it was two African American women because that paper called the women by name and the reporter either knew them or found out who they were. It is possible the *Globe-Democrat* reporter, who also stated John Wheeler's name wrong in the same story, did not know the women and assumed that they were white. *Missouri Republican,* March 21, 1879; *St. Louis Globe-Democrat,* March 21, 1879.

> a systematic rule of behavior towards them, such as ku-kluxism, cross-roads brigades, intimidation, rangers, decoyers, assassins and murderers in all shapes and phases—all for one end—the political, social and moral degradation and destruction of the colored citizens of the Southern States. The system was no sooner conceived and adopted than it was executed, and with such terrible reality that not alone were the bonds of liberty and happiness destroyed and sacrificed, but that greatest of all blessings, life, even was in no way exempted from the rule. . . . which impel the colored citizens of the South to the separation from that land, people and customs of the South, and of which they are natives and to the manor born, to some land in the far West, where homes, protection and security are insured them.

Although the rift between the conservative and activist members of the St. Louis African American community had been temporarily closed, it would open again soon and lead to charges of financial misdeeds on both sides. The split in the St. Louis African American community concerning the Exodus would be repeated on a larger scale nationally, as Frederick Douglass and other conservative African American leaders began to criticize the Exodusters for leaving the South.[12]

On the local level, the Committee of Twenty-Five was working to move the Exodusters to Kansas as quickly as possible. The Transportation Committee booked passage to Wyandotte, Kansas, for 450 Exodusters on the steamer *Joe Kinney* at a rate of $2.50 per person. The Exodusters and members of the Committee of Twenty-Five made quite an impression on a *Globe-Democrat* reporter as they moved down Pine Street to the wharf on the afternoon of March 22. He wrote, "On they came, the committee in front, an unorganized, straggling crowd, pushing against each other in their eagerness, laughing, shouting, crying, and even dancing. Nearly all were merry; the committeemen because they were ridding themselves of a part of their burden; the refugees because they imagined their fondest hopes were soon to be realized." Not all of the Exodusters were happy on that day. Some of the people consoled a young mother who was mourning the loss of the baby that she had buried that morning. Through her tears, she continued to make her

12. *St. Louis Globe-Democrat,* March 21, 1879.

way to the boat. For most, however, joy was the order of the day. As they arrived at the boat, hundreds joined in singing. The lyrics of their song, "Get on board little children, get on board little children, get on board little children, for there's room for many more," seemed to speak to the entire African American population, urging them to leave the South and seek a new life elsewhere.[13]

There were some complications for the Transportation Committee when it tried to provide tickets for this group of migrants. Due to its limited funds, the committee insisted on helping only those Exodusters who could not afford to help themselves. Sometimes, it was difficult for the committee to tell who actually needed their help. Some Exodusters falsely claimed destitution to take advantage of the relief efforts. In one instance, an Exoduster insisted that he did not have a cent, then, just as the committee presented him with his free ticket, he dropped his pocketbook and $800 fell on the ground in front of everyone. He quickly paid for his ticket and boarded the boat. Such displays of wealth were a very rare exception, but still provided ammunition to those who criticized the Exodus.[14]

Another complication came when Willis Carter, self-appointed leader of a group of Exodusters, collected money from sixty or seventy people for tickets without keeping track of who had given him money. When Carter proceeded to pass out the tickets to whoever happened to be near, even if they had not paid, those who had paid him accused him of stealing their money. With a mob surrounding him threatening bodily harm, members of the Transportation Committee stepped forward and led Carter to safety. The members of the committee then raised more funds by passing the hat among themselves and donating their own money to supply tickets to those who had paid Carter and not received tickets. Such haphazard ways of conducting the relief, while noble, opened up the relief workers to charges of not keeping a close eye on accounts.[15]

As the Transportation Committee was securing passage to Wyandotte for the Exodusters, other members of the St. Louis African American community were cleaning the churches in anticipation of more

13. Ibid., March 23, 1879.
14. Ibid.
15. Ibid.

migrants. It was a prudent move, as Exodusters continued to pour into the city. The same night that the *Joe Kinney* left for Kansas, the *Halliday* arrived with several hundred new migrants and the *City of Helena* landed with twenty-five families on board. Fortunately, these Exodusters were better equipped than previous groups. With household goods, some livestock, and money to pay for their continued passage on to Kansas, they would only need to be taken care of until transportation to Kansas became available. The St. Louisans took them to the churches to wait, and provided them with free food and lodging.[16]

It was fortunate that the *Halliday* and *City of Helena* passengers were more self-sufficient than previous refugees, because the St. Louisans who were providing relief were quickly losing ground financially. On March 23 a plea for help went out to the St. Louis community. It read:

> Much needs to be done for the colored emigrants now in the city. The three church congregations that have borne the burden of expense for the last two weeks have nearly exhausted their means, and unless assistance is procured from other sources the result will be disastrous. In order to obtain sufficient means to keep the emigrants fed and sheltered a Relief Committee has been appointed for the purpose of soliciting subscriptions.

William P. Dye chaired the seven-person committee; it also included John W. Wheeler and Moses Dickson. The financial situation was dire enough for the relief effort that Tandy told a reporter the Exodusters should still leave the South and come to St. Louis, but that he wished they would not come so fast and would be more self-sufficient when they arrived. It was quite a different outlook than he had shown at the mass meeting a few nights earlier, but given the pressures that the relief workers were under it is quite understandable.[17]

It was still being reported that thousands of Exodusters were waiting on the riverbanks waiting to be picked up by the St. Louis–bound riverboats. Some Exodusters were reporting that less than one-fifth of those desiring to leave the South had arrived in St. Louis, and the *City of Helena* passengers stated that, had there been room, three times as

16. *Missouri Republican,* March 23, 24, 1879.
17. *St. Louis Globe-Democrat,* March 23, 1879; *Missouri Republican,* March 23, 1879.

many people would have gotten on board. As the boats kept arriving, the numbers of Exodusters in St. Louis kept growing and the pressure on the Committee of Twenty-Five kept increasing.[18]

By March 26 there were more than 2,500 Exodusters in St. Louis, most of them being maintained through the churches by the Committee of Twenty-Five. In less than three weeks of work, the relief workers had spent more than $1,500 on the migrants, the majority of the money coming from the African American community. The *Globe-Democrat* challenged the white citizens of St. Louis to get involved in the relief, stating, "So far, little assistance has been rendered by white people, who must now bestir themselves in this cause, or remain idly by while hundreds of human beings suffer." Unfortunately, this call to action was in vain.[19]

The challenge of the *Globe-Democrat* was by and large ignored by white St. Louisans. In the words of the *New York Times,* the white community looked upon the suffering of the Exodusters "with cold indifference." As donations from the cash-strapped African American community began to slow to a trickle and the Committee of Twenty-Five went deeply into debt, the white community's reluctance to help frustrated the leaders of the relief effort. On March 27, Reverend John Turner, pastor of St. Paul's Chapel, voiced the frustration that all of the relief leaders were feeling. While holding a letter from a small Illinois town that was offering aid for the Exodusters, Turner stated that whites in St. Louis should feel shame because outsiders were offering more help than they were. Turner then tried to appeal to whites on a more practical level, stating that "unless these immigrants are shipped off they will be a heavy burden on the city for a long time to come." Since the white community had assumed little of the burden and therefore was not being inconvenienced by the presence of the Exodusters, the pleas went nowhere.[20]

Reverend Turner's greatest frustration was with white churches in St. Louis, for none of them had given any donations for the Exoduster relief, and had, in fact, ignored appeals for aid. In his interview with the *Globe-Democrat* reporter, Turner explicitly blamed racism for the white

18. *St. Louis Globe-Democrat,* March 23, 25, 1879.
19. Ibid., March 26, 1879.
20. *New York Times,* April 29, 1879; *St. Louis Globe-Democrat,* March 27, 1879.

community's inaction, stating, "They have evinced no desire to be charitable on this occasion, though they should lose all sight of the prejudices which they may have toward our race, and by appealing to their congregations in our cause cement the tie that should bind together all Christians, be they white or black." That white churches had ignored the relief effort particularly stung: "We have received no donations from white congregations, and only one minister has visited me; he was an Episcopalian, a man whom I had never seen before, while the many others with whom I am acquainted have never even sent their cards to me." Turner understood that the refusal to help was symbolic of a deeper racism as he concluded, "Verily, I believe there is yet a strong color line in this city."[21]

On April 4, James Milton Turner, serving as secretary of the Finance Committee, decided to try his luck at asking the white churches for assistance. Perhaps his political status as a "representative colored man" would help. In a circular submitted to the local newspapers, he appealed to the white churches' impulse toward charitable Christianity, while connecting the Exodus with African American freedom. His letter stated,

> You are well-advised through the press of this city that there are hundreds of colored refugees from the South in this city, on their way to a distant home, where they hope to enjoy, for themselves and their children, that freedom which is the inalienable right of man, and God-Given. The great Apostle to the Gentiles, whose teaching you profess to follow, declared that God created all nations of one blood, and that greater than faith or hope is charity. These people are of our race, and look to us to make an appeal to you in their behalf.

James Milton Turner's appeal, like John Turner's appeal weeks earlier, went virtually ignored by the white St. Louis churches; the churches did not see the Exodus as a problem that concerned them.[22]

Despite their frustration and lack of funds, the relief committee continued with their task as best they could. They continued to greet the

21. *New York Times,* April 29, 1879; *St. Louis Globe-Democrat,* March 27, 1879.
22. *St. Louis Globe-Democrat,* April 5, 1879.

new migrants and care for them, aiding some Exodusters for as long as two weeks while arranging their transportation to Kansas. In mid-April the Committee of Twenty-Five contracted with the Missouri River Packet Company to provide transportation to Kansas. The rates of the contract were $3 for each adult and $1.50 for each person between the ages of twelve and twenty-one; children younger than twelve traveled at no cost. Under the terms of the contract, the packet company would also provide the use of their wharf-boat as shelter. It seemed that just as one boatload of Exodusters would be placed upon the Missouri River, another would be landing in St. Louis on the Mississippi. The mind-numbing exercise continued at a furious pace throughout March and April, consuming every spare moment of the Committee of Twenty-Five members' time. John Johnson, the customs house clerk, stated that he would work on Exoduster relief in the mornings before his job began at 9 a.m., and would often attend meetings of the Committee of Twenty-Five that lasted from 7 p.m. until as late as midnight.[23]

Members of the Committee of Twenty-Five would greet the Exodusters as they landed in St. Louis, then lead them to the churches where they would be sheltered. After arranging for the Exodusters' belongings to be secured, the committee members would then document the names of the Exodusters and provide health care, clothes, and food to those in need. The committee members also arranged for the notarized affidavits that allowed many Exodusters to document their stories of ill treatment in the South. Perhaps most important, the relief workers were simply there for the Exodusters, providing friendly faces in a confusing and often frightening situation. The *New York Times* reported, "The colored citizens here are doing their whole duty: but their contributions are largely uncounted, so far as a balance-sheet is concerned, because in the main their charity has been given in the form not of cash paid in hand, but of food, clothing, shelter, and, above all, of loving kindness and deep charity, from which a sympathetic encouragement has flowed." The sense of community between the St. Louis African American community and the Exodusters was clear.[24]

After the Exodusters were settled in their respective shelters, the committee members would then spend their time gathering donations,

23. *New York Times,* April 29, 1879; Voorhees Committee Report, pt. 2, 298–99.
24. *New York Times,* May 10, 1879.

negotiating with riverboat companies, and settling disputes. One thing to remember is that getting the Exodusters on the boats to Kansas was not the end of the process. Since food was not included in the price of passage, the Committee of Twenty-Five also took responsibility for feeding the Exodusters during their trip on the Missouri River. The provisions provided by the Committee of Twenty-Five for a group of 250 Exodusters aboard the *Joe Kinney* steamer bound for Wyandotte, Kansas, is typical of the relief effort. The supply list for the trip included 800 loaves of bread, 238 pounds of meat, three barrels of beans, four barrels of crackers, a barrel of meat, and a barrel of corn meal. During the month of April, an average of 150 Exodusters landed in St. Louis every week, and the weekly expenses for the Committee of Twenty-Five averaged nearly $800. On April 16 the Committee of Twenty-Five reported that more than 6,000 Exodusters had landed in St. Louis since the beginning of the movement; two-thirds of those landing were destitute and dependent upon the committee for food, clothing, shelter, and passage to Kansas. By the end of May, 200 Exodusters were being sent to Kansas every Saturday.[25]

Providing the Exodusters boat passage to Kansas and food for the trip are two indications that the St. Louis Committee of Twenty-Five was concerned with more than just charitably relieving the Exodusters' suffering in St. Louis or getting them out of the city. The committee was dedicated to the idea that the Exodusters would continue their journey to Kansas, and have the opportunity themselves to decide if they wanted to stay. In keeping with their dedication to helping the Exodusters complete their journey, in mid-April the committee sent two of its members to Kansas to evaluate the Exodusters' condition.

Charles Prentiss, one of the more active relief organizers, and Daniel Prince left by rail on April 15 for a three-day trip. What they found in Kansas disturbed them, as they encountered Exodusters in worse conditions there than they had experienced in St. Louis. In Wyandotte, the small town on the Missouri River where most of the Exodusters had been shipped, the two men were met with respect by the mayors of Wyandotte and Kansas City and were invited to attend a meeting of the county council. However, at the meeting, the Wyandotte leaders pleaded

25. *St. Louis Globe-Democrat,* April 21, May 29, 1879; Schwendenman, "Saint Louis and the 'Exodusters,'" 43; *New York Times,* April 17, 1879.

with the St. Louisans not to send any more Exodusters to their city. There were 2,500 Exodusters languishing in Wyandotte, a number nearly equal to the city's population, and the city leaders explained that they did not have the resources to aid so many destitute people. Later, at the end of April, Wyandotte would begin forcibly stopping new Exodusters from landing. In Kansas City a relief committee had been organized, and the committee had begun collecting donations, but the mayors of both Wyandotte and Kansas City had issued proclamations forbidding any more Exodusters to land in their cities. In spite of this proclamation, the mayor of Kansas City, unlike St. Louis's mayor, worked to organize and provide relief to the Exodusters in his city.[26]

Governor John St. John of Kansas responded to the Exodusters arriving from St. Louis by writing a letter to Moses Dickson, letting him know that although the river towns were protesting, the state of Kansas would not allow any Exodusters to be turned away. In Wyandotte Prentiss and Prince realized that the 3,000 Exodusters who had passed through Wyandotte quickly and dispersed into the countryside had found means of earning a comfortable living, but those who remained in the cities were having serious difficulties. The two men resolved to return to Kansas and help the Exodusters complete their journey into the Kansas countryside. Prentiss and Prince returned to St. Louis to take care of new arrivals, but their trip to Kansas had convinced the two men that the Committee of Twenty-Five was doing the right thing and that the work was important and should continue. They remained in personal correspondence with Governor St. John, keeping him informed of the plans of the St. Louis community.[27]

Prentiss and Prince returned to Kansas a week later, over the objections of John Turner, who felt it was too expensive to send two men to Kansas instead of one. On April 25 Wyandotte's mayor, J. S. Stockton, and its city collector, William Albright, together with Kansas State Senator W. J. Buchan traveled to St. Louis to meet with Moses Dickson and other St. Louis relief workers. The Kansans persuaded the St. Louisans that Wyandotte was not the best place for the Exodusters to

26. *New York Times,* April 17, 29, 1879; *Kansas Pioneer,* April 26, 1879; Grenz, "The Exodusters of 1879," 54.

27. *St. Louis Globe-Democrat,* April 10, May 14, 1879; *New York Times,* April 29, 1879; Papers of John P. St. John, Kansas State Historical Society, Topeka.

land, that its resources were tapped out, and that Kansas had established a Central Distributing Center for the Exodusters in Topeka. Convinced, the St. Louis committee shipped the next group of Exodusters to Topeka and Lawrence instead of Wyandotte.[28]

Meeting the arrivals in Kansas, Prentiss and Prince expanded the role of the St. Louis relief organization. Prentiss took charge of the Exodusters when they landed in Kansas and arranged for them to disperse quickly to new homes. By May 10 he was traveling with other Exoduster groups to their new homes, helping them complete the final leg of their journey. The St. Louis relief committee was now no longer just offering relief for the Exodusters who were stranded in St. Louis; it was clearly aiding them in completing their migration. The St. Louis relief efforts had moved beyond charity for the people who were showing up on the St. Louis riverfront to encouraging the migration from the South, helping the migrants through St. Louis and on to Kansas, and then aiding the Exodusters in Kansas as well.[29]

The expanded role of the committee meant that money would become an even more difficult issue, but even before Prentiss and Prince went to Kansas, the committee was suffering financially. The Committee of Twenty-Five, realizing that their appeals to help from the St. Louis white community were being ignored, began to seek donations from throughout the country as a means of continuing their work. In a letter addressed "To all Generous and Charitable People Throughout the Country" that appeared in the *New York Times* on April 3, the desperation of the committee is evident. The letter states, "The colored people of this city are doing all in their power to help them. So far, they have fed and sheltered them while here and have forwarded several hundred to Kansas, but still they come, and we are now compelled to appeal to generous and benevolent persons everywhere to aid us in our work. We need both money and clothing. In the name of God and humanity we ask aid for the refugees." Throughout the month of April, the committee made repeated appeals to the nation.[30]

Their calls for help were finally answered as donations of food, clothing, and money began to arrive from individuals across the North.

28. *St. Louis Globe-Democrat,* April 26, 1879; *New York Times,* April 27, 1879.
29. *St. Louis Globe-Democrat,* April 29, May 11, 1879.
30. *New York Times,* April 3, 1879.

By May 10 the *Times* was reporting, "Of nearly $1,500 received by the Committee of Twenty-Five up to this date, the major portion has come from elsewhere than in St. Louis, or even in Missouri." The *Globe-Democrat,* in keeping with its qualified support of the Exodus, established a Refugee Relief Fund that served as a clearinghouse for donations that were being made by individuals to newspapers in the North. The establishment of the fund made the *Globe-Democrat* a significant presence in the financing of the relief effort. A report given on April 21 by the Committee of Twenty-Five's financial section stated that of the $608.18 collected since the previous meeting, $323.35 had come from donations collected through the *Globe-Democrat*'s relief fund. The newspapers donating to the *Globe-Democrat*'s fund included New York's *Times, Herald, Tribune, Evening Post,* and *Mail,* the *Detroit Post* and *Tribune,* the *Indianapolis Journal,* and the *Cincinnati Commercial,* whose editor sent forty dollars of his own money for the Exodusters.[31]

The *Globe-Democrat* also printed lists of the donations received by the leaders of the Committee of Twenty-Five. These lists give a good indication of the breadth of support for the Exodus outside of St. Louis. One fairly typical entry lists the donations received by John Turner between April 10 and April 22:

> Rev. George H. Hann, Peoria, Ill. $10.14; B.A. Imes, Oberlin, Ohio 5.00; Rev. G.H. Graham, Zanesville, Ohio 32.50; M. Friede, St. Louis, Mo 5.00; Rev. Thomas A. Check, Dubuque, Ia 4.20; W. Gladstine, White Cottage, O 10.00; V.W. Pratt, New York, N.Y. 1.00; Mr. Payne, Pana, Ill 1.00; Rev. J.T. Nease, Edwardsville, Ill 7.15; G.H. Hann, Peoria, Ill 46.00; Rev. Edward Epps, Naperville, Ill 5.00; John B. Martin, Cincinnati, O 5.00; Bryan Carter, Keokuk, Ia 10.75; J.K. Hilyard, St. Paul, Minn 23.00; C.B. Allyn, Brooklyn, N.Y. 19.23; Ira W. Russell, Keene, N.H. 5.00; W.R. Daun, Ottumwa, Ia 5.00; Daniel Roberts, Burlington, Vt 10.00; H.W. Chapman, Hillsboro, N.H. 2.00; M.J. Francis, Wilmington, Del 2.50; B.W. Arnett, Columbus, O 100.

The presence of ministers in the list, and the listing of one minister, George Hann, twice with two different donations, indicates that groups

31. *St. Louis Globe-Democrat,* April 12, 13, 19, 22, 1879; *New York Times,* April 21, May 10, 1879.

as well as individuals were sending money to the Exodusters. Also, the amount of some of the contributions—$32.50, $19.23, and $10.75, for example—indicate collections taken among communities and congregations in the North to help the Exodusters.[32]

Many former abolitionists played roles in organizing relief efforts in Northern cities. On April 4, James Milton Turner had written in a letter to the editor of the *Globe-Democrat* that the Committee of Twenty-Five had not "received any assistance in their work from any abolition or other society outside of St. Louis," but the lack of assistance from former abolitionists was soon to change. By the end of the month groups across the North had begun to organize. One week after Turner's letter, two groups from the old abolitionist stronghold of Oberlin, Ohio—the Ladies' Missionary Society and the Second Congregational Church—had each sent three barrels of secondhand clothes to St. Louis. In Philadelphia, many members of the African American community gathered on April 8 in the A.M.E. church to raise money for the St. Louis Exodusters. Ten days later, the Historical and Literary Association of the church sent $107 and a box of clothes. After the A.M.E. church led the way, the Philadelphia African American community began taking up a general collection to forward to St. Louis. The white community in Philadelphia followed suit; on May 2 Philadelphia's mayor appointed a committee of twenty (including a former governor) to solicit aid for the Exodusters. It was eventually reported that a Philadelphia Quaker donated the formidable sum of $10,000 to aid Exodusters who had made it to Kansas but who were suffering.[33]

As news of the Exodus spread, African Americans in the North and their supporters began to see the Exodus as a momentous event that could define American race relations in the post-Reconstruction era. The *New York Times* wrote, "No single thing has occurred since emancipation and enfranchisement which proves as thoroughly that the negro is striving to fit himself in the best sense for freedom, its cares and responsibilities equally with its rights and advantages, as this wonderful movement of a whole race, this effort to get where, as one of the refugees said, *people will not be angry because we strive to send our children to school"* (italics in original). The ability to send children to school

32. *St. Louis Globe-Democrat,* April 23, 1879.

33. Ibid., April 4, 9, 15, 19, May 3, 1879; *Topeka Tribune,* July 8, 1880.

speaks to a belief that the children have a chance at a brighter future than their parents. In the post-Reconstruction South, the brighter future was dimming; in Kansas, the Exodusters hoped that it would be restored. Governor St. John of Kansas agreed, stating that the Exodus was "the second emancipation, and under it we want to make the blacks absolutely and forever free." Symbolically, the Exodus was taking on meaning far beyond the simple migration of a few thousand people.[34]

The St. Louis Committee of Twenty-Five reinforced that symbolism by continually framing their requests for aid in terms of freedom and liberty. In one appeal, the committee wrote, "To the humane and liberty-loving people throughout the country: The colored refugees from the South, fleeing from oppression and inhuman treatment, continue to arrive at our wharf daily." The liberty-loving people of the North responded to such requests. The New York African American community came together April 10 in a mass meeting at the Zion A.M.E. Church, where a thousand people braved pouring rain to show their support for the Exodusters. During the meeting, entrepreneur and activist George T. Downing gave an address in which he condemned Southern persecution of African Americans and stated that the African American community would do everything in its power to "assist our native brethren struggling to be free." At the same meeting, Reverend W. F. Dickerson stated, "From this time forth there is no lethargy for colored men until right to the negro triumphs over might. They stand beside the grave of their liberty. The promises of the South to them are no longer believed. The whipping post is again erected, and in Georgia the chain gang exists anew." A week later, the New York committee that was formed at the meeting released a public appeal that touted the Jeffersonian ideals contained in the Exodus. The appeal stated, "The whole land will ultimately be enriched by a movement which seeks to make a free yeomanry out of a class of dependant wage laborers."[35]

Other cities joined in the movement to help the Exodusters escape from the South. Milwaukee formed a group—the E. Gillespie Colored Relief Society—that sent $350 to John Turner in late April; a similar committee was formed in Davenport, Iowa, with the purpose of helping

34. *New York Times,* May 20, July 11, 1879.

35. *St. Louis Globe-Democrat,* April 17, 1879; *New York Sun* quoted in the *St. Louis Globe-Democrat,* April 13, 1879; *New York Times,* April 11, 21, 1879.

"colored people who leave the South for Kansas and Northern States." A committee was formed in Decatur, Illinois, to raise funds for the Exodusters, and forwarded $157 to the St. Louis Committee of Twenty-Five. On April 14 the African American community of Cincinnati gathered at the Union Church to gather contributions and appoint a committee to aid "the suffering negroes at St. Louis."[36]

The belief that the Exodus was a movement to secure liberty for African Americans was reflected in statements made by relief contributors. An anonymous donor from Michigan who sent $100 to aid the Exodusters enclosed a note that read, "The unprotected wards of our nation are leaving their old homes in search of freedom." In Dayton, Ohio, a principal of an African American school wrote of the Exodus, "We regard the exodus as a providential act, and we stand ready to give all the aid possible. God bless the movement and hasten the glorious cause." By June, a meeting in Boston of Exodus supporters included a speaker who stated that Southern leaders were plotting another war over the Exoduster issue. To enthusiastic applause, the Bostonians then passed a series of resolutions declaring it the federal government's duty to ensure that laws were observed and African Americans retained the right of travel without restraint.[37]

The support in the North was due in part to a trip made by Charlton Tandy in April and May. On April 12, Tandy left for Washington, D.C., intent on meeting with President Rutherford B. Hayes and other leading Republicans to present them with the affidavits taken from the Exodusters testifying to Southern bulldozing. Another purpose of the trip was to travel throughout the East to raise awareness of the Exodus and collect funds for Exoduster relief. Tandy's trip got off to a poor start. Most local white St. Louis Republicans had not aided the Exoduster relief efforts, but had begun to realize that the Exodus was not going to stop anytime soon. With a goal of gaining federal assistance for the Exoduster relief, they provided a memorial for Tandy that would indicate that he had their support.

After arriving in Washington, Tandy called on Frederick Douglass, whom he had met many times before in St. Louis, in hopes that Douglass would provide him with an introduction to the president. Douglass,

36. *St. Louis Globe-Democrat,* April 14, 19, 29, 1879; *Kansas Pioneer,* April 19, 1879.
37. *St. Louis Globe-Democrat,* April 12, 17, 1879; *New York Times,* June 25, 1879.

however, rudely refused, claimed he did not know Tandy, and told him to "get some old-time abolitionist to introduce you." Douglass opposed the Exodus on the grounds that in his opinion, things were getting better for African Americans in the South, that their labor made them valuable and that whites would soon recognize that, that it was the government's job to protect African Americans in the South, and that the Exodus would make African Americans compete with white farmers and laborers in the North. In trying to facilitate the Exodus, Tandy was, in Douglass's view, making a harmful mistake for African Americans. After being rebuffed by Douglass, Tandy turned to R. T. Greener, the African American dean of Howard University, for help.[38]

Greener was a strong supporter of the Exodus, and he offered introductions to not only the president but also many other leading national Republicans. Tandy stayed in Washington for eleven days, twice meeting with Hayes. The president stated his support for Tandy's mission, but offered no federal assistance to either aid the Exodusters or stop the bulldozing. Greener also gained Tandy entrance into a forty-member Republican caucus that included Senators Roscoe Conkling, James Blaine, and William Windom. After Tandy spoke at the caucus and presented the Exoduster affidavits to the senators, they offered their strong support and gave him an endorsement to carry to the Northeast. After Tandy's trip gained publicity in the eastern newspapers, Frederick Douglass contacted Tandy and asked for a meeting. The request drew a dismissive response from Tandy, who told Douglass to "go to the devil."[39]

From Washington, Tandy traveled to Philadelphia, where he was met by the mayor and presented with a $1,400 contribution. Traveling to New York, Tandy spoke at a meeting at the famed Cooper Union. The meeting, which the *New York Times* called "the largest assemblage of colored people ever seen in this City," featured speeches by Abraham Lincoln confidant Thurlow Weed and African American leader Henry Highland Garnett. When Tandy spoke, he talked about Douglass's response to his request for aid, reporting that Douglass disapproved of the Exodus entirely. The mention of Douglass's opposition drew hisses from the crowd, and then Tandy had a joke at Douglass's expense. He stated that upon hearing the advice that the Exodusters stay in the South,

38. *St. Louis Globe-Democrat,* May 16, 1879; Douglass, "The Negro Exodus," 39–43.
39. *St. Louis Globe-Democrat,* May 16, 1879; *Missouri Republican,* May 16, 1879.

Tandy questioned why Douglass himself did not stay in the South. The question drew laughter from the crowd.[40]

From New York, Tandy traveled to Massachusetts, where his relief work was praised on the floor of the state government. In Boston, Tandy attended a meeting of Exodus supporters at historic Faneuil Hall. The meeting was organized and managed by African American members of the Boston community, and was attended by some of Massachusetts' most prominent white citizens, including the governor and William Lloyd Garrison. The meeting had the feel of an old-time abolition meeting, with women playing a prominent role on the stage and whites in the South serving as targets during indignant speeches. The large crowd frequently cheered the speakers, who were, in the words of the *New York Times,* "extremists who have all along opposed the conciliatory policy toward the South." Tandy gave a very well-received speech in which he recounted the horrors of Southern bulldozing. The meeting passed resolutions showing support for the Exodusters and appointed a committee to secure donations for the cause. The crowd and Tandy perhaps recognized that the crisis might offer the chance to control and reshape the South in the wake of the failures of Reconstruction.[41]

Tandy's tour through the East brought much needed attention to the Exodus and secured nearly $2,000 for the relief effort, but he did not escape criticism. Tandy, though reasonably well known in St. Louis and Missouri, was not a "representative colored man" who was recognized outside of his city. As Painter notes, two New Orleans papers painted Tandy as small-time, agreeing with Frederick Douglass that he was a mere ward politician who was unpolished and in over his head in the loftier circles that he encountered during his trip. The papers also accused Tandy of trying to advance his own cause at the expense of the Exodusters, a charge that Senator Daniel Voorhees would later make during Senate hearings investigating the causes of the Exodus. When confronted with these charges during the Senate hearings, Tandy vociferously denied them, claiming that he was not out for personal gain and had only aided the Exodusters because it was his duty. None of the

40. *St. Louis Globe-Democrat,* May 11, 1879; *New York Times,* April 24, 1879.
41. *St. Louis Globe-Democrat,* April 25, May 16, 1879; *New York Times,* April 25, 1879.

Northern papers that covered Tandy's trip commented negatively on his character or his presence, and all reported that his speeches were well received.[42]

The criticisms of Tandy as being unpolished and minor mirrored the schism that had grown between two factions of the St. Louis Committee of Twenty-Five during the month of April. James Milton Turner served on the finance committee of the Committee of Twenty-Five. Turner, easily the most prominent African American in St. Louis, if not the most well-liked, had never been as convinced of the need for the Exodus as many of his counterparts. In late March he had publicly questioned the propriety of helping the Exodusters because he feared that offering them aid would encourage more people to leave the South. His position was at odds with many other leaders who were actively working to achieve just such a result. Ever image-conscious, he may also have worried about the picture of African Americans that the destitute and uneducated Exodusters embodied. In a letter to the editor of the *Globe-Democrat* on March 23, Turner had called the Exodusters "spendthrifts" who were "without frugal habits" and who reminded him "more of grown up children than of persons of mature mind." With this opinion he aligned himself with many in the white community who viewed the Exodusters in much the same way, as unthinking people who had been tricked and were easily misled on a fool's errand to Kansas.[43]

Although he continued working for Exoduster relief, by mid-April Turner was questioning the finances of the Committee of Twenty-Five, charging that the committee was unorganized and irresponsible and that all finances had not been accounted for by committee members who were receiving donations. Turner felt that the relief effort should be run as a business venture with white support as opposed to a charitable effort organized through the African American churches. In spite of some of his earlier rhetoric and unlike others involved in Exoduster relief, Turner never viewed the Exodus as a life-and-death struggle. As

42. Painter, *Exodusters,* 226–28; Voorhees Committee Report, pt. 2, 62.

43. *St. Louis Globe-Democrat,* March 26, 1879; Donald G. Nieman, ed., *Church and Community among Black Southerners: 1865–1900,* 51.

Gary Kremer writes, "To them [the Exodusters], the exodus meant an opportunity to live the kind of life that had been denied them in the South—an end in itself. To Turner it was, first of all, a way of changing that life-style and, second, a concrete way of demonstrating black power in the South—both means to an end." On April 15, Turner incorporated the Colored Immigration Aid Society, a for-profit organization dedicated to raising funds for the establishment of African American colonies in the West. The society's goal would be to solicit funds to buy land in the West, and then to sell that land to potential settlers for a profit. Ideally, the society would help settlers who were worthy (in other words able to pay for land) and discourage migration of those who were not willing or able to independently survive on the Western plains.[44]

At the society's first meeting, held on April 19 at the Lindell Hotel, Turner invited three white politicians, Jacob E. Merrell, William Scudder, and Edward Rowse, to advise the new organization. The men's questions indicate the level of ignorance that many in the St. Louis white community had about the Exodus. Although the Exodus relief had been continuing for more than a month and the newspapers had almost daily stories of the Committee of Twenty-Five, one of the first questions asked by the white advisers was if there were any organizations in the city working on Exoduster relief. When the advisers asked Turner if he thought the Exodus would continue, Turner stated that while he did not encourage the Exodus, he felt that it would continue and that by fall "every last Negro in the South would have folded his tent and stolen away."[45]

The Committee of Twenty-Five came in for some pointed criticism during the meeting; it was stated that the original committee was jealous of the new organization and would not cooperate or compromise. After singling out Moses Dickson and John Turner for denigration, Turner stated that he wanted white involvement in his organization to "place the Association on a responsible basis before the public." Turner insisted in stating that the Committee of Twenty-Five was receiving money, and people were questioning where it was going. At the end of

44. *St. Louis Globe-Democrat,* April 20, 1879; Kremer, *James Milton Turner,* 115; *New York Times,* April 19, 1879.

45. Kremer, *James Milton Turner,* 113; *St. Louis Globe-Democrat,* April 20, 1879.

the meeting, it was agreed that there would be a black board of directors and a white advisory board of prominent citizens (including prominent businessman and Assistant Secretary of the Treasury A. G. Edwards) that would give the new organization credibility.[46]

The Colored Immigration Aid Society met again at the Lindell two nights later, but only ten people showed up for the meeting and none of the white advisers attended. For an organization that was determined to be held accountable for managing donations properly, the society got off to a bad start. Turner, when announcing donations, stated that he had received $107 from Philadelphia, and "$20 or $25 (he forgot which) from a gentleman named Thomas." The main order of business was hearing a statement from Charles Starkes, who was serving as treasurer of the Committee of Twenty-Five. He stated that Reverend John Turner, Reverend Moses Dickson, and others were bypassing him in violation of the original organized structure of the committee. Instead of turning donations over to Starkes and then withdrawing money as needed, the members of the Committee of Twenty-Five were handling donations themselves. Turner implied that the members of the Committee of Twenty-Five had not accounted for nearly $2,000 of donations, and he stated that the Committee of Twenty-Five had, "without authorization, gone into organization, was collecting money without any responsibility, and disbursing it without obeying the rule made by the mass meeting or noticing the Treasurer at all."[47]

Starkes was probably correct in stating that the members of the Committee of Twenty-Five were haphazard when it came to accounting for donations, but Turner was wrong in implying that the members of the committee were stealing. The Committee of Twenty-Five had organized rather quickly but, considering the circumstances, this was understandable. When donations had begun appearing from outside of St. Louis, the committee had made sure to submit records of the contributions to the *Globe-Democrat,* which ran regular reports of the group's finances. Instead of malfeasance, it was most likely a case of expedience and necessity; the Exodusters were landing so fast, and help was needed so quickly and on such a large scale, that John Turner,

46. *St. Louis Globe-Democrat,* April 20, 1879.
47. Ibid., April 22, 1879.

Moses Dickson, and others felt it was necessary to use whatever money was at hand rather than to spend time following procedures. The practice may have provided immediate help to some Exodusters, but it opened the relief workers up to charges of fraud and theft.

After the Colored Immigration Aid Society's initial meeting, word spread through St. Louis that James Milton Turner was raising suspicions about the finances of the Committee of Twenty-Five. The committee was not about to take quietly the accusations from its rival. A meeting was held at St. Paul's Church during the afternoon of April 21, the same day that James Milton Turner's group held their second meeting. The ostensible purpose of the Committee of Twenty-Five's meeting was to form a permanent organization to replace their original ad-hoc organization, but responding to James Milton Turner's accusations became the order of the day. One of the first orders of business was to account for any money that the Committee of Twenty-Five had received. It was reported that $606.16 had been collected, with $323.35 coming to the committee through the *Globe-Democrat.* Of that total, $328.35 had been paid to the Missouri River Packet Company for transportation, and $150.74 had been spent on provisions. Charles Prentiss stated that he had received $1 donations from two different men and that these donations had been presented to the committee.[48]

The Reverend John Turner was chairing the meeting, and he reported that two men, the Reverend S. P. Anderson and James Milton Turner, had both been in receipt of goods and money but had not turned in the donations. After some debate, it was determined that Anderson had acknowledged the donations and was planning on turning them in, but it was noted that James Milton Turner had been receiving donations but had made no report for nearly two weeks. During the meeting, J. T. Smith, who was not a member of the Committee of Twenty-Five, asked to be allowed to speak. He stated that James Milton Turner had asked him to go to the meeting to try to bridge the divide between the two groups. His statements and his presence upset some members of the committee, who indicated that it was a private meeting and that he was not welcome. Charles Prentiss stated that James Milton Turner was still a member of the committee and had not had the com-

48. Ibid.

mon courtesy to submit a resignation before leaving to start his own organization.[49]

John Turner and Moses Dickson were particularly upset with James Milton Turner. John Turner took the floor and stated that he would like a union of the two organizations, but "if Milt Turner and the others wanted to go off and set up a kingdom for themselves they could do so. This committee was the trunk; a limb might fall off, but that would not hurt." The work was of too great a magnitude, John Turner insisted, to let James Milton Turner damage what they were trying to accomplish. John Turner stated that by starting his own organization, James Milton Turner had "put his foot in it," and now he had to go on alone. Others in the meeting echoed John Turner's feelings; they stated that since James Milton Turner had his foot in it, "let him sink." John Wheeler, who was normally moderate in his views, said that James Milton Turner was the "Judas of the Committee"; he had betrayed them and they would have nothing more to do with him. Although other committee members took offense at Wheeler's strong condemnation of James Milton Turner, during the ensuing vehement debate Wheeler continued to stand by his statement.[50]

Although James Milton Turner's accusations went too far for the committee's liking, they did spur it to form a permanent organization, the Colored Refugee Relief Board.[51] The Reverend Moses Dickson was elected president of the new board, John H. Johnson was its secretary, Reverend John Turner was treasurer, Charles Prentiss was chairman of the important Transportation Committee, and Charlton Tandy was to serve on the board of directors. The board eventually established permanent offices at 903 Morgan Street and rented a building on the levee in an attempt to house Exodusters and give some relief to the crowded churches. Moses Dickson would pay half of the $15 a month rent for the office since he would use it for both his private and relief business. The building on the levee was rented for $8 a month and would hold in excess of 150 people in its five rooms. The establishment

49. Ibid.

50. Ibid.

51. On April 28, the board took the official name of "The Colored People's National Board of Immigration of the City of St. Louis, Mo.," but continued to be commonly called the Colored Refugee Relief Board.

of the permanent organization did little to quell the firestorm of accusations that were flying back and forth between the two groups.[52]

On April 24, James Milton Turner wrote a letter to the editor of the *Globe-Democrat* stating his belief that the other relief leaders were too insignificant to take seriously. He wrote, "I desire to state that I will henceforth treat with contemptuous silence all innuendoes leveled at me by men who are scarcely known beyond their own family circle, and who, through a spirit of envy, jealousy or malice, belabor themselves to pervert my motives and endeavors in behalf of my poor afflicted people, and to detract from my well-earned reputation and character in this country." Directly below Turner's letter was a letter calling for an investigation of Turner's charges against the Committee of Twenty-Five. The next day, 200 people showed up at Turner Hall to discuss the charges against the committee. Charles Starkes made a report reiterating his earlier claims that Charles Prentiss, John Turner, and others had not followed proper procedures in either collecting or disbursing money for the Exodusters. The assembled group appointed a committee of five men to investigate the Committee of Twenty-Five and compel them to make a full report of their activities. When the five-man investigative committee later made an appearance before the original relief committee, they were told that the Committee of Twenty-Five had nothing to hide and that its books were open for anyone to examine at anytime.[53]

The same day that James Milton Turner and others were meeting to investigate the Committee of Twenty-Five, the newly formed Colored Refugee Relief Board was meeting with the Kansas representatives in a meeting mentioned earlier. At the meeting, the Kansans informed the Colored Refugee Relief Board that having two relief groups in St. Louis was going to cause confusion for people and would probably hurt donations. Gustavus St. Gem and Meyer Rosenblatt, two white St. Louis Republican officials who had taken an interest in the Exodus, were present at the meeting. Rosenblatt told John Turner and the others, "The seeming wrangle between the two committees has a bad effect in New York and throughout the entire East. Persons there want to send money and don't know whom to send it to; they don't know which is

52. *St. Louis Globe-Democrat,* April 26, 29, 1879; Athearn, *In Search of Canaan,* 30.
53. *St. Louis Globe-Democrat,* April 24, 26, 29, 1879.

the right committee. This other committee may get $500 or so, which should have been received by you. This other committee should cease to exist." Of course, the members of the Colored Refugee Relief Board agreed that they should be the only relief organization.[54]

Charlton Tandy, who was on tour through the East during much of the conflict between the two organizations, was told numerous times by people in the East that the existence of two boards in St. Louis was hindering donations. St. Gem had a similar thought, stating, "The fact that there are two organizations in the city tends to have a bad effect, and as soon as possible one ought to be done away with. I am of the opinion that this, the original committee, is the one to be relied on, it should be supported by our citizens and confidence should be placed in it by colored people." That night at a mass meeting, the Colored Refugee Relief Board decided to apprise the Kansas Relief Board of plans to send any Exodusters to Kansas. In an attempt to establish their legitimacy as the true relief organization in St. Louis, the board also voted to establish official communications with relief boards in cities throughout the East.[55]

In a raucous if somewhat sparsely attended meeting at Turner Hall on May 6, the Colored Refugee Relief Board made its case to the St. Louis African American community. Reverend Moses Dickson, newly elected president of the board, made a presentation that traced the growth of the relief organization from the founding of the Committee of Twenty-Five through the Colored Refugee Relief Board. Dickson stated that when the original relief effort was organized, he felt that the need was going to be temporary, but he then changed his mind and felt that the need for Exoduster relief was going to be great for some time.[56]

Dickson then read a report that explained the board's activities from its founding on March 17 to May 3. He stated that 50,050 rations had been issued, with the St. Louis African American community donating most of the food. There had been 13,500 pieces of clothing donated to the Exodusters, with four-fifths of the donations coming from cities in the North and East. The number of Exodusters who had arrived and received care from the board was 5,169, only 1,526 of whom had been

54. Ibid., April 26, 1879.
55. Ibid.; *New York Times,* April 27, 1879.
56. *St. Louis Globe-Democrat,* May 7, 1879.

adults. Furthermore, Dickson stated, the board had a list of full names of the heads of families of those who had been helped. Of the 5,169 Exodusters who had been helped, 5,004 had been sent to Kansas, with the remaining 164 still in St. Louis waiting for transportation. There had been $4,705.36 in cash donated; of that amount St. Louisans had donated $1,201.25. The board had paid out $4,527 in transportation and incidentals, leaving $178.28 in the treasury. At the end of his report, Dickson let his temper show, saying that if there was any dissatisfaction, "let any sorehead show his hand," reminding the crowd that while other folks were talking, his folks were working. There were many objections to Dickson's comments, and people in the audience began shouting and hurling personal insults at one another. Eventually, Dickson's report was accepted, and the Colored Refugee Relief Board remained as the primary relief organization in St. Louis. They were continually aware of perceptions of financial impropriety; in May Moses Dickson issued a warning to the public that the relief organization "has no authorized agents for the purpose of soliciting funds for the refugees. All persons representing themselves as soliciting agents of the Board are declared imposters. Donations of money or clothing should be sent to the Board's office."[57]

James Milton Turner's organization continued limping along for a few months, but it never achieved any real success. Its only tangible contribution to the Exodusters was a $250 donation it made to the Colored Refugee Relief Board in the summer of 1879. By donating to the organization he had shunned, perhaps James Milton Turner was trying to mend fences or retain influence within the African American community. Most likely it was a combination of the two. Whatever the intended purpose, the donation did not heal the rift between leaders of the two groups. During the U.S. Senate's Voorhees Committee inquiry in 1880 into the Exodus, John Johnson, who had known Turner since boyhood, would claim that Turner's organization was a speculative money-making scheme where donations would be used to purchase lands in the West, then the land would be sold to colonies of Exodusters on the installment plan.[58]

After the failure of his organization, Turner came out against the Exodus, stating that the South was the true home of African Americans

57. Ibid.

58. Kremer, *James Milton Turner*, 115; Voorhees Committee Report, pt. 2, 295.

and that the commercial interests of the country demanded that African Americans stay in the South and let the racial problems work themselves out over time. With this argument, Turner echoed the thoughts of Frederick Douglass, who also understood the reasons the Exodusters were leaving the South, but argued that African Americans should stay in the South and try to establish their rights slowly. Echoes of this same argument would be heard short decades later as Booker T. Washington, Henry McNeal Turner, and W. E. B. DuBois debated the best strategy of African American liberation.[59]

On May 4, Douglass presented a lecture before a racially mixed audience in Baltimore. During his three-hour talk, Douglass conceded that the Exodusters' lot in the South had been a hard one. He agreed that they had been subject to violence and intimidation, and had been deprived of their rights. He also conceded that their political rights would be safer in Kansas. However, Douglass argued that seeking relief through migration was a mistake, for in the West, African Americans would have to compete with German and Irish immigrants for jobs, while in the South they could leverage their usefulness as labor. African Americans were better off in the South than they were fifty years earlier, Douglass maintained, and they would be better off in the South in another fifty years. In actuality, African Americans in the South fifty years after Douglass's speech would still be in a difficult position—denied political opportunity, socially segregated, and economically exploited. It would take another migration, this one much larger and longer than the Exodus to Kansas, to permanently change American demographics and contribute to an end to overt white supremacy in the South.[60]

Douglass's feelings about the Exodus were well known when Tandy returned from his eastern tour. During Tandy's tour, Douglass had written a letter to the *Philadelphia Times* accusing Tandy of using the Exodus to gain political popularity. At a mass meeting at the Eighth Street Baptist Church on May 15, Tandy presented a report of his trip, and in the report he mentioned that Douglass had treated him coldly and had refused to assist him in presenting his mission to the president. At the end of his speech, Tandy spoke out again against Douglass, and said that Thurlow Weed, Wendell Phillips, and William Lloyd Garrison

59. Voorhees Committee Report, pt. 2, 288–95; Cox Richardson, *The Death of Reconstruction,* 171; Douglass, "The Negro Exodus," 40–50.

60. *New York Times,* May 5, 1879.

openly condemned Douglass to Tandy. Douglass's name drew hisses from the crowd; one member rose and proposed a resolution condemning Frederick Douglass and naming him as a traitor to his race for not assisting Tandy in his mission of helping the Exodusters.[61]

At this point, James Milton Turner, who attended the Colored Refugee Relief Board meetings to play the devil's advocate role, rushed to the platform demanding to be heard. "My friends, my friends, think what this means," said Turner, who argued that passing a resolution condemning Frederick Douglass would make the St. Louis African American community look too extreme. In a speech that the *Globe-Democrat* called "highly eulogistic" of Douglass, Turner begged the people to withdraw the resolution. Turner said that Frederick Douglass had done more for African Americans, and that it would be a shame if St. Louis African Americans condemned him before investigating any charges against him.[62]

When told he was out of order, Turner refused to take his seat, continuing to talk through the confusion and cries of "set Turner down" from the audience. After Tandy came forward and said that although everything said about Douglass was true, he did not support the resolution, the resolution was tabled. When it was withdrawn, Turner shouted, "This is the happiest moment of my life, this prevention of a wrong to Douglass and the colored race." The next day in a meeting of the Colored Refugee Relief Board's officers, Prentiss and Tandy both gave speeches that were highly critical of Douglass and others who were against the Exodus. Echoing his popular line from his eastern speech, Tandy stated, "If Douglass and others were against the Exodus and in favor of the colored people remaining in the South and fighting it out, why didn't they go down there and help them fight it out?" Prentiss called the author of a resolution that was against aggressive movement to aid the Exodusters "a coward and a villain," and proposed a resolution to condemn Douglass. Over the objections of Reverend John Turner, it passed. However, cooler heads eventually prevailed and the resolution was never made public.[63]

As the St. Louis relief groups aided the Exodusters and argued amongst themselves, St. Louis business leaders and Southern planters

61. *Missouri Republican,* May 16, 1879; *St. Louis Globe-Democrat,* May 16, 1879.
62. *Missouri Republican,* May 16, 1879; *St. Louis Globe-Democrat,* May 16, 1879.
63. *Missouri Republican,* May 16, 1879; *St. Louis Globe-Democrat,* May 17, 1879.

had been working to stop the Exodus by forcing the packet boats to ignore the thousands of African Americans lining the shores of the Mississippi. Some planters threatened boycotts of any packet lines that picked up Exodusters, and some threatened violence against the boat captains. There were places along the river where captains dared not pick up the waiting Exodusters for fear of being killed. One riverboat executive admitted that twenty-five leading merchants of St. Louis had presented him with a petition to make the passage rates on the Mississippi high enough that Exodusters could not afford passage. In the late spring and summer of 1879, the price for passage to St. Louis increased to five dollars, and children under age twelve were no longer free. Dogs no longer were granted free passage either.[64]

The refusal to pick up the Exodusters did not last long, only about a month, but it lasted long enough to significantly halt the Exodus as the Exodusters used up what little resources they had waiting in vain on the riverbanks. Riverboat captains who were worried about breaking the federal laws that governed common carriers found ways around the law. One first mate reported, "We brought thirty of the refugees. We could have brought a thousand if we would have taken them. If we have thirty deck-passengers on board, the law cannot touch us for refusing more." The Exodusters left on the riverbanks were slowly seeing their hope of escaping the South drift away. As Painter notes, the momentum of the movement was broken by this delay, and the most intense period of the Exodus was over.[65]

As they waited for the riverboats, the Exodusters faced continual harassment from the bulldozers, planters, and authorities. Some tried to put up fences to keep the bulldozers out; others had their livestock and belongings taken away until they promised to remain in the South. George Halliday, who later received medical care, food, lodging, and passage from St. Louis to Kansas, related to Frank Fletcher the difficulty that he had in trying to leave the South. He stated, "They tried to prevent my coming north. The deputy sheriff came on the boat at 'Hard Times,' and took away from me a pair of mules. He had a constable and twenty-five men with guns to back him. I got on the boat ten miles below there." Halliday was part of a group of twenty people who traveled through St. Louis. Although he had little more than the

64. Athearn, *In Search of Canaan,* 146; Cohen, *At Freedom's Edge,* 181.
65. Fletcher Report, 15; Painter, *Exodusters,* 196–200.

clothes he wore, he knew that he was lucky to escape the South before it was too late.[66]

Exoduster supporters had no way of knowing that the high tide of the Exodus was ebbing, but they were worried. The existence of two relief committees in St. Louis and the reports of Exodusters stranded on Southern riverbanks had caused concern from benefactors in the East. In May, Philadelphia Quakers sent Thomas Conway, a well-known African American Radical Republican leader, to St. Louis to assess the situation. Conway had strong connections to the national Republican leadership; he had been part of a meeting held at William Windom's home in April to devise a plan to help African Americans leave the South. Conway had picked up the honorary title of "General" when he worked for the Freedmen's Bureau during Reconstruction, and he was a polarizing figure. Southerners and many northerners called him a con man, but northern radicals praised him as a tireless worker for African American causes. Conway arrived in St. Louis and met with members of the Colored Refugee Relief Board. Conway was long acquainted with Reverend John Turner, and he explained to the St. Louisans that people in the East were reluctant to donate since they did not know which relief organization was legitimate.[67]

Conway explained that the cause of the lull in the Exodus in recent weeks was the refusal of the riverboat companies to pick up the Exodusters. Most riverboat lines other than the Anchor Line had denied the Exodusters, and even the Anchor Line had recently stopped picking up the travelers as well. At the beginning of the Exodus, the Anchor Line, which did not want to lose its business with the Southern planters, had offered to take Exodusters back South free of charge, but few could be convinced to accept the offer. In June, the Anchor Line was blamed for supporting the Exodus and was the subject of a $10,000 lawsuit brought by a Mississippi landowner. The landowner claimed that since the Anchor Line usually carried freight, not passengers, it was overstepping its bounds by providing rides to the Exodusters. In an attempt to defend his company from "wicked lies" and "false statements" by whites who were against the Exodus, the president of the Anchor Line, John Scudder, wrote a public letter stating, "All of the interests of the

66. Fletcher Report, 16–20.

67. Athearn, *In Search of Canaan,* 135–47; *St. Louis Globe-Democrat,* May 12, 1879.

Anchor Line, and of each of its owners, are so closely identified with the prosperity of the Southern country that they would be false to themselves if they would do anything that would impair the business sources of the people who live in that country." To reinforce that he was only following the law, Scudder continued, "Not one negro—man, woman or child—has come to St. Louis on any of the boats of the Anchor Line at less than the regular established rates." Under continual pressure from the white community, Scudder finally decided that his company would ignore the Civil Rights Act and, like the other riverboat lines, would refuse to provide transportation to the Exodusters. With this decision, the entire migration was threatened. To try to ensure the continuation of the movement, Conway told the board of his plan to charter armed riverboats to go down the Mississippi River and rescue the Exodusters who were waiting on the shores. Conway used his connections to get a meeting with President Hayes for himself and Reverend John Turner.[68]

At the meeting, Conway and Turner described the Southern bulldozing to a sympathetic Hayes and told him of their plans. Hayes told the pair that any attempt to stop the riverboats by bulldozers was a violation of the law, and that the government should protect boats on a national highway. Encouraged, and thinking that Hayes was indicating the military might get involved to protect the riverboats, Conway continued with his plans. However, after visits from outraged Mississippi and Louisiana congressmen, Hayes soon backtracked. He insisted that boats should have the right to travel the Mississippi River unmolested, and that any American should have the right to migrate from one part of the country to another. However, the president also stated that he never said that the boats of Conway's plan would have protection. Furthermore, Hayes said he thought it would be unfortunate if large numbers of African Americans were to concentrate in one area. Presumably, he meant if African Americans were to concentrate in one area outside the South, since more than 90 percent of African Americans were living in the states of the former Confederacy.[69]

Conway's plan was never realized, but his threats worked. Faced with the possibility of the federal government coming down against the

68. Athearn, *In Search of Canaan,* 15; *St. Louis Globe- Democrat,* May 16, June 28, 1879.
69. *St. Louis Globe-Democrat,* May 29, 1879.

bulldozers, the packet boats resumed picking up any Exodusters who were left on the riverbanks. Unfortunately, the interdiction had irreparably damaged the Exodus; the Exodusters who had waited for the boats had been put back to work by the Southern landowners. As Painter writes, "only the physical impossibility of keeping body and soul together during the long wait broke the back of the Kansas Fever Exodus." For all intents and purposes, the Kansas Fever Exodus was over.[70]

Although the migration to Kansas continued steadily for the next two years, the urgent rush out of the South had subsided. The St. Louis African American community continued helping migrants who came through their city, but most of the later travelers to Kansas were more self-sufficient than their predecessors. Increasingly, as they realized that the Southern economy was not going to be threatened by African American migration to Kansas, the white community of St. Louis relaxed their opposition to the Exodusters and some even helped with relief for those who were in need. When Charlton Tandy testified at the Voorhees Committee hearings in 1880, he carried a statement of support for the migration by white St. Louisans, although most of the signatories were Republicans.[71]

When the need was greatest in the spring of 1879, however, the St. Louis African American community was the group that stepped forward and helped the Exodusters. In their willingness to provide the Exodusters with not only charity but also hope of reaching Kansas and achieving their freedom, the St. Louis African American community worked for freedom for all African Americans. They realized that the Exodus of 1879 was not just about a small group of penniless people migrating to a new place, but about Americans deciding for themselves what their future would be.

70. Painter, *Exodusters,* 200.

71. Voorhees Committee Report, pt. 2, 42.

4

The Red Sea

I have not the means to get to Kansas.
I will have to work here until I get
the money or my friends help me.
— J. D. DANIEL, EXODUSTER

The hardships of the post-Reconstruction South had finally forced the Exodusters to leave their homes and seek a better life in the West. Kansas in particular held a special allure to those fleeing Southern oppression at the end of Reconstruction. It was, in the words of one Republican newspaper, "the State that was settled for an idea. That idea was freedom for the slave—the right of the colored man, equally with the white man, to own the soil and enjoy the fruits of his labor."[1] The state known for its abolitionism had long been a focus of African American dreams; words of encouragement and welcome from whites in Kansas made the state an even more appealing destination. The *Lawrence Journal* took pride in Kansas's reputation, stating, "There is something infinitely honorable to the state of Kansas that its name has become the synonym of freedom all over this land so that the oppressed turn their eyes toward us as they used to toward the north star." Senator John Ingalls of Kansas indicated that one hundred thousand Exodusters would be welcome in his state, while Governor John P. St. John promised equal protection under the law. In a letter that numerous newspapers printed, St. John wrote of the Exodusters, "As for Kansas, I

1. *St. Louis Globe-Democrat,* March 27, 1879.

think I speak the sentiment of the people when I say that they shall never be turned from our doors for want of bread."[2]

St. John then related the Exodus to breaking the power of the Southern elite by writing, "As for myself, I believe that God's hand is in this work and that the present Exodus from the Southern States is one of the means used by Him to forever cement the American Union and to render secession in the future impossible." Editorials from papers like the *Lawrence Tribune,* which stated, "Kansas has good rich land in plenty for all who will cultivate it without regard to race, color or previous condition of servitude," served to further convince more Exodusters that there was a Promised Land in the Midwest. As mentioned previously, as the Exodus grew in strength, many white Kansans, especially those in the Exoduster-saturated town of Wyandotte near the Missouri border, would protest against the Exodus. However, most Kansas state leaders and many everyday Kansans took steps to provide for the Exodusters until they could be distributed to areas around the state. For a time, Governor St. John personally led the early relief efforts, and aid associations were organized in many parts of the state. Compared with the South, Kansas, despite the cold weather and the hardships, seemed welcoming to the Exodusters.[3]

African American migration to Kansas had been building for a decade, and in the years preceding the Exodus of 1879 there had been a few successful migration efforts. Benjamin "Pap" Singleton, who called himself the "Moses" of the Exodus, had, for ten years, successfully led groups of African American colonists from Tennessee to various areas of Kansas. Additionally, the nearly all-black town of Nicodemus was founded in 1877 by African Americans from Kentucky. Nicodemus became the most famous African American town in Kansas, and is still in existence today, although it has rapidly declined since its heyday in the 1880s. After arriving at the Nicodemus site, its colonists went to work building sod houses, dugouts, and frame structures in which to live, while sharing resources like plows and livestock. After their first

2. Cohen, *At Freedom's Edge,* 168–97; *Lawrence Journal* quoted in the *New York Times,* April 29, 1879; Hartzell, "The Negro Exodus," 727; *Philadelphia Times* quoted in the *St. Louis Globe-Democrat,* May 13, 1879.

3. *Philadelphia Times* quoted in the *St. Louis Globe-Democrat,* May 13, 1879; *Lawrence Tribune* quoted in the St. Louis *Globe-Democrat,* April 13, 1879; *Kansas Pioneer,* May 3, 1879.

crop was harvested, they became a self-sustaining community. That venture, the Singleton colonies, and other existing African American settlements served as evidence of possible success to the Exodusters. Even unsuccessful efforts, like the attempt to colonize Cherokee County in southeast Kansas, still kept the dream alive for many in the South. However, as mentioned previously, the migration of 1879, the Exoduster migration, was not an organized colonization effort; it was characteristic of an escape.[4]

As the Exodusters attempted figuratively and literally to move from slavery to freedom, they were dependent upon aid from the St. Louis African American community to complete their journey. Fortunately, African Americans in St. Louis were exceptionally qualified to serve as a bridge over the Red Sea, to serve as a conduit between slavery and freedom. The St. Louis African American community was in a unique position to help the Exodusters, but the city's social, economic, and political climate presented distinct challenges for the Exodusters as well. St. Louis, being neither exclusively Northern nor exclusively Southern, reflected its distinctiveness in the area of race relations. This distinctiveness allowed a margin of freedom within which the African American community could achieve a measure of citizenship that was not available to African Americans in most Southern cities.

Previous studies of the Exodus have not placed the relief within the context of African American resistance. Robert Athearn's book, *In Search of Canaan,* is an excellent overview of the Exodus, but although his book dedicates a chapter to discussing the St. Louis relief efforts, he does not sufficiently discuss the reasons behind the efforts and does not sufficiently contextualize them within St. Louis history. Instead, Athearn explains the motivation for the relief efforts in terms of charity, writing that African Americans in St. Louis "were less inclined to ponder the origins of the movement. They knew something of southern political conditions, but they also knew that they were in no position to do much about it. . . . they offered to help, much in the manner of volunteer firemen who respond to an emergency, by giving what aid they could as fast as possible."[5]

4. Painter, *Exodusters,* 150–56; *St. Louis Globe-Democrat,* May 2, 1879; Cohen, *At Freedom's Edge,* 171; Richard Cordley, "The Advancing Exodus"; Gary R. Entz, "Image and Reality on the Kansas Prairie: 'Pap' Singleton's Cherokee County Colony," 136–39.

5. Athearn, *In Search of Canaan,* 18.

I agree with Athearn that originally the support offered by the St. Louis African American community was simply relief, and members of the community did act as "volunteer firemen." However, I contend that as the St. Louis African American leaders realized the importance of the movement, they recognized the role that the Exodus played to all African Americans and organized their relief efforts in large part because of this realization. The relief leaders did also, in fact, think about the origins of the movement and stated so many times. They discussed it in meetings, they testified about it to Congress, they interviewed the Exodusters and had their statements notarized, and they attempted to publicize those reasons in newspaper interviews and public announcements. While it is true that they felt they could not go to the South and change the conditions there, relief leaders did think that the Exoduster movement was a way to change Southern society. By removing themselves (and their labor) from the South, the Exodusters were threatening the economic system that supported Southern white supremacy. By helping the Exodusters escape, the relief leaders were striking a blow against the Southern power structure. The leaders of the St. Louis relief efforts were civil rights activists who had been working for years to improve the lot of African Americans in St. Louis, in Missouri, and in the United States. They viewed Exoduster relief as another opportunity to secure rights for African Americans.

Nell Irvin Painter devotes a portion of her classic book, *Exodusters,* to the St. Louis relief efforts, but St. Louis is not the focus of her study. Instead, she concentrates on the origins of the Exodus and discusses how it was a response to the experiences of African Americans during and after Reconstruction. Glen Schwendemann, in his article, "St. Louis and the 'Exodusters' of 1879," gives an overview of the St. Louis relief efforts and places them somewhat within a larger, national framework. However, Schwendemann does not explore the importance of St. Louis as a city, nor does he connect the Exoduster relief with other civil rights activities by the relief leaders. A deepening of our understanding of both the St. Louis relief efforts and the members of the St. Louis community who organized the relief for the Exodusters will also broaden our understanding of the Exodus, and contribute to our understanding of African American nineteenth-century civil rights activity.

Throughout the nineteenth century, immigrants to the United States and white Americans viewed the West as a place for economic opportunity and spiritual rebirth. From the Jeffersonian vision of an idyllic land peopled by yeoman farmers to the present-day growth of western states, Americans have always moved to the West to build new lives. Many white Americans believed in the West as a place of economic, spiritual, and social rebirth and autonomy, and their beliefs were often proved correct in their experience. African Americans held this view of the West as well, regarding it as a place to escape racism and gain economically. But while African Americans had been present in the West for generations, unfortunately they were not often able to take full advantage of its offerings.[6]

The West was a place of opportunity, but it was also a land of economic, social, and racial inequities, containing, as Eric Foner reminds us, "indentured Indian labor, Mexican-American peonage, and work under long-term contracts for Chinese immigrants." During the antebellum period, white Americans and European immigrants were encouraged to populate the West, but much of the West was officially closed to African Americans. Western states including Indiana, Illinois, Missouri, Iowa, and Oregon had "black laws" that either specifically prohibited African Americans from entering their territory, fined African Americans who were in their territory, or had other restrictive laws against African Americans. Oregon passed an African American exclusion law in 1857 that was not officially repealed until 1927. Since many African Americans in the antebellum period were effectively blocked from moving to the West as a way to improve their economic status, they were blocked from a key factor of economic development. After the Civil War and the end of chattel slavery, many African Americans were eager to take advantage of newly available land and opportunities in the West like their white counterparts had been doing for generations.[7]

African Americans added another layer to the American view of the West: they saw it not only as a place of economic opportunity and spiritual rebirth but also a refuge from the racial restrictions that existed in the South and East. To historian Quintard Taylor, the central paradigm in the history of African Americans in the American West is contained

6. Henry Nash Smith, *Virgin Land: The American West as Symbol and Myth,* 4–12; Quintard Taylor, *In Search of the Racial Frontier: African Americans in the American West, 1528–1990,* 81; William Loren Katz, *The Black West,* 1–142.

7. Katz, *The Black West,* 55; Eric Foner, *The Story of American Freedom,* 75–77.

in the following questions: "Did the West represent the last best hope for nineteenth and twentieth-century African Americans? Was it a racial frontier beyond which lay the potential for an egalitarian society? Or did the region fail to match the unobtainable promise imposed upon it by legions of boosters, to provide both political freedom and economic opportunity?" Taylor goes on to note that African Americans may have exaggerated the potential of the West as a region separate from the racial oppression of their experiences in the East and South.[8]

The Exodusters personified the African American vision of the West and the struggles that Taylor's questions contain. They based their movement on hope, faith, and a belief that in the West they would finally be beyond racial bounds and would be treated as equals, but in their movement they exaggerated the economic possibilities that the West had to offer them. Although in Kansas they had a sympathetic government, private aid, and less political and economic terrorism than in the South, the state was still not the panacea for racial oppression of which many Exodusters dreamed. Ultimately, Kansas failed to live up to many of their expectations and their movement only gained limited tangible successes, but the Exodusters' search for an American home existing outside of American racism continues to be instructive.

The Exoduster movement was among the first signs to the outside world that many African Americans were unhappy in the post-Reconstruction South and were seeking a permanent home elsewhere. The St. Louis African American community, like the rest of the nation, was surprised by the suddenness and size of the movement, and of the destitution and determination of the migrants. The sudden movement of Exodusters in 1879 was both leaderless and unplanned, an unorganized response to Southern conditions. Instead of saving money and acquiring supplies that would help a colonization attempt, the dangers and economic difficulties of the South led many Exoduster families to simply sell what belongings they could to finance their trip.[9]

Painter calls the Exodus of 1879 a millenarian movement, arguing that the Exodusters of 1879 were moved to migrate in an unorganized fashion and were convinced of both the righteousness and ultimate success of their movement regardless of the conditions. In making

8. Taylor, *In Search of the Racial Frontier,* 17–81.
9. Painter, *Exodusters,* 4; Athearn, *In Search of Cannan,* 5.

this argument, she is rightly and carefully differentiating between the colonies of well-supplied, well-organized migrants of previous and later migrations to Kansas and the pell-mell rush of penniless freedpeople who showed up in St. Louis in the spring of 1879. William Cohen also marks the difference between the Exodusters of 1879 and earlier colonies, although he stops short of agreeing with Painter that the movement was decidedly millenarian. Cohen does, however, agree that "the Exodus of 1879 had elements of mass hysteria and precipitous flight" indicative of millenarianism even though it was not a strictly millenarian movement. Whether the Exodus of 1879 was a strictly millenarian movement is unclear; what is clear, however, is that the Exodusters of 1879 were fleeing the South out of fear—they feared bulldozers, political violence, and economic intimidation that would leave them virtually enslaved.[10]

The Exodus of 1879 that passed through St. Louis came from a localized base—the Louisiana parishes of Madison, Upper Tensas, East Carroll, Ouachita, and Richland and the Mississippi counties of Hinds, Issaquena, and Washington contributed most of the Exodusters. Collectively, this was known as the "bull-dozed" district, where political and economic intimidation of African Americans following Reconstruction was commonplace. Whites in that district used every means possible to stop the Exodus. On more than one occasion, Greenville, Mississippi, Exodusters were dispersed by order of the mayor. In that same city, at least one man was arrested for inciting the Exodus and held on a $250 bond. In Vicksburg, Mississippi, a leading citizen proposed issuing African Americans scrip instead of money as a way of keeping them economically tied to the area. Playing on the fears of a Yellow Fever epidemic, Vicksburg also admonished St. Louis that any African Americans entering St. Louis from Vicksburg should be subject to a rigid sanitary inquiry.[11]

Violent intimidation, however, was also a common method of stopping the Exodus in the South. Exoduster John Cummings stated, "there are four or five hundred up on Little Deer Creek who cannot get out; they won't let them come on the boats; they won't let them leave without a pass; they will be killed if they try to get out without a pass."

10. Cohen, *At Freedom's Edge,* 176; Painter, *Exodusters,* 180.

11. *New York Times,* March 24, April 3, 16, 1879; *St. Louis Globe-Democrat,* May 24, 1879.

Exodusters spoke about sneaking out at night, leaving all of their belongings behind so as to not attract the attention of the bulldozers. Edward Leonard, a twenty-four-year-old Exoduster from Warren County, Mississippi, stated, "The white people didn't want us to come away; tried to stop us; they took away everything they could from 'em. I had a horse and some hogs, and they took my horse away; I didn't owe them anything; they claimed I owed. A man came and took my horse away by force; he was not an officer of the law." Daniel Parker of Delta, Louisiana, spoke about fleeing without his family. He said, "my wife and two children are down in Madison Parish; I had to leave without them; If I had tried to start with them there would have been a fuss; there was a large crowd of people on the bank, and after they found out the colored people were going to leave they took all the bedclothes and things they could from them; the land-owners in the South did everything they could to prevent us from leaving." Thomas Carroll reported that two men in his party were arrested before they could leave, and one other man was killed as he waited on the riverbank. One Exoduster's fears of the tightening restrictions in the South were made clear when he stated to a St. Louis newspaper reporter, "I don't think my people will ever get out of the South because the people are getting so bad. The white people at first said they didn't care how many negroes left the South, but when they saw so many leaving they are doing everything in their power to prevent it."[12]

Although white settlers who moved to the West were celebrated for their pioneer spirit and individualism, to many outside observers it was inconceivable that rural, Southern African Americans would have the initiative and ambition to leave the South and travel great distances into the unknown in search of a better life. Many people, including Frederick Douglass, held the belief that African Americans had a greater love of home than white Americans and thus were less likely to leave without being coaxed or coerced. The *New York Tribune,* in an article titled "Causes of the Exodus," describes an Exoduster and states, "it is no wonder that he is deceived by false hopes of a freer and better life in the far West, and *conquering the love of home, which is much stronger in the black race than the white,* sells his mule and his plow, and, with his wife

12. Voorhees Committee Report, pt. 2, 48–61; Haviland, *A Woman's Life-Work,* 492.

and children and scanty household effects, embarks on a passing steamer to seek a land of liberty and law"[13] (italics mine).

An April 26, 1879, article in *Harper's Weekly* stated, "The question why they are going is one of peculiar interest, and the first fact shown by the movement is that they are greatly discontented. They are not a nomadic race, and they are satisfied with little. So general flight shows that they are seriously suffering, or seriously alarmed." Douglass, in an article for *Frank Leslie's Illustrated Monthly* in January 1880, wrote, "The colored race is a remarkably home-loving race. It has done little in the way of voluntary colonization. It shrinks from the untried and the unknown. It thinks its own locality the best in the world. Of all the galling conditions to which the negro was subjected in the days of his bondage, the one most galling to him was the liability of separation from home and friends." Douglass goes on to argue that even when enslaved, African Americans would be "partially content" because of a love of home. Of course, as Tandy noted, Douglass himself left home and escaped to the North when his own enslavement became unbearable and he had opportunity to leave.[14]

At the time of the Exodus, there were many theories about why the Exodusters were leaving the South. It was determined by some people, especially Exodus opponents, that the Exodusters were either pawns of Northern Republicans and were being tricked into moving west for political reasons, or were being induced to move west by railroad companies and land speculators. It was believed that only through such trickery could a nonmigratory people be compelled to leave home. One of the earliest articles about the Exodus appeared the day after 280 Exodusters arrived in St. Louis aboard the *Colorado.* The article appeared in the March 12, 1879, edition of the Republican *St. Louis Globe-Democrat,* and had the headline "Duped Darkies," with a subheading, "They are Made Victims to Glowing Advertisements and Fictitious Free Land."[15]

The *New York Times* published one article headlined "A Heartless Hoax," and another *Times* article quoted Democratic Senator Benjamin

13. *New York Tribune* quoted in the *St. Louis Globe-Democrat,* March 21, 1879.

14. *Harper's Weekly,* April 26, 1879; Frederick Douglass, "The Negro Exodus from the Gulf States," 42.

15. *St. Louis Globe-Democrat,* March 12, 1879.

Jonas of Louisiana, who also believed the Exodusters had been duped. Jonas repeated the oft-stated explanation that the railroad companies were enticing the Exodusters: "Glowing stories of this country [Kansas] have been told them by the agents of Western railroads having land to sell, and they naturally want to leave their present homes, where there is hard work and small pay, for this land of peace and plenty."[16] What is problematic with Jonas's theory of railroads enticing the Exodusters of 1879 is that few of the Exodusters had money to buy land; many believed that the federal government would supply them with free transportation, land, and funds to cover start-up costs.

Other Democrats were convinced that the Exodus had far more odious political implications than railroad profits. Indiana, which had previously been a Republican state, had voted Democratic in the 1876 election, but by a very slim margin. When, at the end of 1879, a few hundred African American migrants from North Carolina began appearing in Indiana, Indiana Democrats accused Republicans of shipping them to the state in hopes of tilting its population back to a Republican majority. The movement from North Carolina to Indiana is ancillary to the Exodus that passed through St. Louis, but it should be noted that the Democrats' suspicions about the Indiana migration had some merit. Highly ranked Republicans, including relatives of Rutherford Hayes and members of his cabinet, worked through the National Emigration Aid Society to ultimately send between 2,500 and 3,000 African American migrants to Indiana.[17]

The National Emigration Aid Society was formed in Washington, D.C., in March 1879 to regulate emigration out of the South and to the West as a reaction to the exodus from Mississippi and Louisiana that passed through St. Louis. Although the society claimed that it was willing to send African American migrants out of the South to wherever they desired, in reality, its entire transportation allotment was used to move African Americans from North Carolina to Indiana. Hayes believed that migration of African Americans from the South, whether sponsored or not, was an opportunity to "force the better class of Southern people to suppress the violence of the ruffian class, and to protect the colored people in their rights." Hayes's simplistic view of the situation

16. *New York Times,* March 14, 1879
17. Athearn, *In Search of Canaan,* 212–14.

was that the "better class" of white Southerners (meaning the wealthy ones) was innocent of attempting to control African American laborers, and that the violence was randomly committed by the white working class. This view of racial violence in the South being random rather than the foundation of an entire system of white supremacy was one shared by many other Northerners. This belief would hinder African American advancement in the South until the modern civil rights era dismantled the structures of the South's segregated society.[18]

The Exodus to Kansas that passed through St. Louis was much more spontaneous than the Republican-supported migration from North Carolina to Indiana. Any political organizing or benefits from the Exodus for the Republicans came about after thousands of Exodusters decided, on their own, to leave the South. The Republicans' best argument against the Kansas Exodus being a Republican plot was a simple one: why would the Republicans send thousands of voters to Kansas, a state that was already solidly Republican? Shipping African American Republicans to states that were politically in flux was much more advantageous as a matter of political strategy. However, in the minds of many people, especially many Democrats, Republican involvement in the movement to Indiana was proof enough that all African American migration out of the South was a Republican plot. Although the Exodus to Kansas was not a result of a Republican conspiracy, most Republicans did come to support the Exodus for a variety of reasons. Heather Cox Richardson's argument that the "Exodusters reaffirmed the Republican belief in the efficacy of agriculture as the basic occupation of individuals in America's political economy" is sound.[19]

The Exodusters believed that owning land in Kansas would provide them with freedom not available in the South. An African American newspaper argued that dispersing the African American population would weaken Southern landowners' hold on African American labor and serve as an antidote for racial problems. A year after the Exodus, the editors of the paper believed that the migration was not yet large enough and should continue. They stated, "There are altogether too many of us at the South. Labor is too plentiful. Capital too domineering.

18. Cohen, *At Freedom's Edge,* 189–93; Davison, *The Presidency of Rutherford B. Hayes,* 221.

19. Cox Richardson, *The Death of Reconstruction,* 164.

Scatteration should be the word. Not to Kansas alone, but all over the North, save its great cities. Agricultural in their capacities, let our brethren seek the farming regions of the great North and the greater West and all will be well." This proved to be somewhat prophetic as the "scatteration" of a later, greater migration enabled African Americans to assert political and economic power.[20]

Republican Senator William Windom of Minnesota was an ardent supporter of African American migration out of the South, and he eventually became president of the National Emigration Aid Society. In January 1879, before the Kansas Fever Exodus had begun, Windom introduced a resolution urging Congress to form a committee to investigate the possibility of encouraging African American migration out of the South. Although the resolution did not pass and said nothing about federal aid to help migrants, it did spark talk of a mass migration. William Cohen argues that Windom's resolution was the "ray of hope" that the Exodusters needed to start heading north. It is no coincidence, he notes, that Exodusters expecting federal aid arrived in St. Louis less than two months after Windom's resolution. Cohen argues that it was rational of the Exodusters to expect government help, because the Freedman's Bureau had set a precedent of government assistance to former slaves. Furthermore, the bureau had supported African American migration to Florida under the Southern Homestead Act.[21]

Heather Cox Richardson notes that many northerners believed the Windom resolution and the threat of a new Louisiana constitution that could take away the gains of Reconstruction were the reasons behind the Exodus of 1879. Painter also argues that the Louisiana constitution was a factor. In addition, she argues that the Kansas Fever idea had taken hold as early as 1875 in Tennessee, and by 1878 existed in other parts of the South. She points to a letter written to President Hayes from an African American teacher who migrated from Mississippi to Kansas in 1878. The teacher represented acquaintances who also wanted to migrate. In his letter, he asks Hayes for government assistance in three areas: transportation, subsistence and shelter for a year, and tools. These are, Painter notes, the same three needs that the Exodusters of 1879 ex-

20. *Philadelphia Christian Recorder,* March 10, 1881; *Philadelphia Christian Recorder,* December 16, 1880.

21. *New York Times,* April 7, 1879; Cohen, *At Freedom's Edge,* 176–81.

pected the government to provide. Windom, Painter says, felt that his resolution did not cause the Exodus, and most importantly, she adds, no Exodusters interviewed mentioned Windom or the resolution. Most likely, the Exodus was a combination of all of the reasons given—bulldozing, the taking away of political, economic, and social freedom that had been gained in the years after the Civil War, rumors of federal help, and the promise of Kansas.[22]

Almost from its beginning, Windom had been calling for a congressional investigation into the causes of the Exodus as a way to expose Southern political terrorism against African Americans, but he had been unsuccessful in getting the hearings approved. In response to the Indiana migration and charges that it was politically based, Senator Daniel Voorhees, an Indiana Democrat, decided to use hearings to expose the Exodus as a Republican political ploy to import votes. The five-person committee that was formed in January of 1880 was officially called the "Committee to Investigate the Causes which have led to the Emigration of Negroes from the Southern to Northern States," but it became commonly known as the Voorhees Committee after Voorhees was appointed its chair. The Democrats held a three-to-two majority on the committee, which interviewed 159 witnesses, lasted four months, and cost an estimated $30,000. Northerners recognized the Voorhees Committee as a Democratic tool to be used in the 1880 election, and thus had low expectations for its conclusions. St. Louisans Charlton Tandy and John H. Johnson were called to testify, affidavits from Exodusters were submitted as evidence, and some Exodusters personally testified. The conclusions of the committee were as expected: the Democrat-written majority report blamed much of the migration on Republican political maneuvering and the Republican minority report blamed the Exodus on political and economic oppression of African Americans at the hands of Southern Democrats.[23]

Although the findings of the report were inconclusive and no one was satisfied with the committee's partisan outcome, many newspapers carried daily, detailed reports of its witness testimony. An important result of the committee's effort, then, was that it gave the Exodusters and

22. Cox Richardson, *The Death of Reconstruction,* 157; Painter, *Exodusters,* 178–80.

23. Cox Richardson, *The Death of Reconstruction,* 173–82; Athearn, *In Search of Canaan,* 208–24; Cohen, *At Freedom's Edge,* 195; Voorhees Committee minority report, ix.

their supporters a voice and allowed them to tell their story to a national audience. Through these reports, many people across the nation were, for the first time, hearing the Exodusters' story of what life was like for African Americans in the post-Reconstruction South. The chilling stories they heard exposed the racial oppression that was occurring on a daily basis. Much of the Exoduster testimony came in the form of affidavits that were collected and supplied by members of the St. Louis relief organization.

It is important to understand why the St. Louis African American community felt so connected to the Exodusters, and why the city of St. Louis proved to be such a difficult barrier for them to cross. Previously, there has been very little written research dedicated to the St. Louis African American community in this specific time period, but some work has been done by historians Lawrence O. Christensen, Lorenzo J. Greene, Gary R. Kremer, Antonio Holland, Judy Day, and M. James Kedro. Christensen contends that although Missouri was a slave state, African Americans in St. Louis were in a relatively stronger position than Southern African Americans during the antebellum period. Although antebellum St. Louis had strict racial codes that denied most rights to free African Americans, the irregular enforcement of those codes left room for some African Americans to succeed, especially financially.[24]

African Americans in St. Louis before the Civil War were able to attain a level of community development that African American communities in other slave-holding cities could not match. This stronger position during the antebellum period essentially gave African Americans in St. Louis a head start when compared to other, more Southern African Americans. Christensen compares St. Louis to Raleigh, North Carolina, Montgomery, Alabama, Richmond, Virginia, Atlanta, Georgia, and Nashville, Tennessee—all cities studied by Howard Rabinowitz in his classic *Race Relations in the Urban South: 1865–1890.* Christensen found that St. Louis African Americans were able to play an important role in state politics, establish churches, start schools, and build a social infrastructure much earlier than African Americans in other slave-holding cities. This infrastructure would prove to be invaluable as thousands of Exodusters descended upon the city and looked to the African American community for help. The response to the crisis was quick,

24. Christensen, "Black St. Louis," 23–25.

wide-ranging, and ultimately effective as the St. Louisans called upon every resource at their disposal to aid the refugees. Fortunately, the African American community was well established in St. Louis.[25]

Cyprian Clamorgan's 1858 text, *The Colored Aristocracy of St. Louis,* is a testament to the development of the African American community in St. Louis before the Civil War. In the book, Clamorgan profiled free African Americans, many of whom had estates worth tens of thousands of dollars and who owned significant amounts of property. Although lamenting the racial inequality that plagued St. Louis, Clamorgan also maintained that through the power of their wealth and connections many free African Americans in St. Louis were able to assert themselves politically. Clamorgan writes, "It will be seen by the following pages that the colored people of St. Louis command several millions of dollars; and every one knows that money, in whose hands soever it may be found, has an influence proportionate to its amount. Now, although our colored friends have no voice in the elections, they are not idle spectators . . . they are not slow in making friends with those who are able and willing to serve them."[26]

The aristocracy profiled in Clamorgan's book were strong supporters of abolition, and Clamorgan notes that "there is not a colored man in our midst who would not cheerfully part with his last dollar to effect the elevation of his race." Although, as Julie Winch, editor of a recent edition of Clamorgan's book points out, "few of the people he [Clamorgan] wrote about assumed leadership positions in the African American community of St. Louis after the war," the stage had been set to use the political strength that wealth and connections afforded them. This strength allowed African Americans in St. Louis to block many of the most devastating characteristics of segregation after the war, and to gain even more political power. This is not to say that the St. Louis African American community had anything approximating equality in St. Louis. However, African Americans in St. Louis were able to effectively wield what little power they did possess.[27]

It was not only the "colored aristocracy" who benefited from the power they had before or after the Civil War. In 1865, as Radical Republicans

25. Nieman, *African Americans and the Emergence of Segregation,* 37–50.
26. Cyprian Clamorgan, *The Colored Aristocracy of St. Louis,* edited by Julie Winch, 47.
27. Ibid., 19–47.

attempted to push through a new state constitution, ninety-four leading African Americans from St. Louis submitted a petition asking for the right to vote. To aid their cause, St. Louis African American leaders and their white allies formed the Missouri Equal Rights League, an organization dedicated to securing civil rights for all African Americans. The Equal Rights League would prove a strong platform for African American leadership in Missouri, providing future African American leaders with valuable experience and connections.[28]

Blessed with more organization, more money, and more freedom than African Americans elsewhere in Missouri, St. Louis African Americans were in the forefront of working for rights for all African Americans in their state. This was necessary, because segregation and white supremacy often did not distinguish between African Americans in terms of economic class or skin complexion. Consequently, despite differences and conflicts within the African American community, the free St. Louis African American elite "often realized that divorcing themselves from the black masses amounted to racial suicide, and they recognized that their political struggle for equal rights in a hostile American society was inextricably bound to the 'uplift' of the entire race."[29]

The same attitude prevailed during the Exodus as members of St. Louis's African American elite recognized a commonality with the penniless refugees from the South despite their myriad differences. The belief that if one African American was denied rights based on race, then all African Americans were at risk greatly influenced the Exoduster relief effort as well as other civil rights activity in St. Louis. The St. Louis African American leaders often worked for the good of the entire race, rather than for gains for specific groups of African Americans. This is not to say that there was not tension between the various groups, or that there was not a strain of elitism that ran through the St. Louis African American community; there was. More importantly, the St. Louis African American leaders recognized that there was an element of white society (including racially based laws) which did not make distinctions among African Americans. Working for the good of all African Americans was a necessity. The influence that African Americans in St. Louis wielded meant that some of the effects of segregation were mitigated. Using the Rabinowitz model of African Americans

28. William E. Parrish, *A History of Missouri,* 147–50.

29. Greene, Kremer, and Holland, *Missouri's Black Heritage,* 71–72.

moving from exclusion from society to segregation within society, St. Louis African Americans, in the words of Lawrence Christensen, moved "from semi-exclusion to semi-segregation rather than from exclusion to segregation."[30]

Although it might be a distinction of degrees, it is still an important distinction to make. For it was within this expanded level of freedom and within their existing social infrastructure that the African American community in St. Louis found the means to aid the Exodusters of 1879. One important element of the infrastructure was the development of churches. The St. Louis African American community, in contrast to African Americans in other slave-holding cities, had well-formed churches, one of which had a congregation of more than one thousand before the Civil War. Many of these churches had African American ministers and extensive property holdings as well. The church provided many things, perhaps most importantly "a source of stability and social strength in an otherwise hostile society." The churches also "provided one of the few forums in which potential black leaders could develop and refine their leadership skills."[31]

Churches in African American communities were more than just places of worship. An African American church was "a bulletin board to a people who owned no organs of communication, a credit union to those without banks, and even a kind of people's court." African American churches in St. Louis, like other African American churches in the South, provided a structure and became centers of civil rights activity and community-building. Aldon Morris argues that since many other societal institutions were either hostile or at best ambivalent toward African Americans, the African American church became the dominant African American institution. Churches "provided the organizational framework for most activities of the community—economic, political, and education endeavors as well as religious ones." It was the African American community, working through these well-established churches, that formed the core of the Exoduster relief efforts in 1879 and 1880.[32]

30. Nieman, *African Americans and the Emergence of Segregation,* 38.

31. Parrish, *A History of Missouri,* 146; Nieman, *African Americans and the Emergence of Segregation,* 38–39; Greene, Kremer, and Holland, *Missouri's Black Heritage,* 68.

32. Taylor Branch, *Parting the Waters: America in the King Years 1954–1963,* 3; Raymond D'Angelo, ed., *The American Civil Rights Movement: Readings and Interpretations,* 149.

As has been noted, St. Louis was a pivotal part of the Exodus story, and St. Louis relief efforts played a vital role in helping the Exodusters complete their journey. Understanding, then, the context within which the St. Louis African American community formed its relief efforts is valuable to Exoduster scholarship. Athearn and other scholars explain much of the St. Louis relief efforts in terms of charity, and one can see that charity to help desperate people was an important motivating factor. However, another overlooked objective is that the relief effort itself became a form of resistance to segregation and white supremacy. If limiting the movement of one group of African Americans threatened the freedom of all African Americans, then African Americans in St. Louis were reinforcing their own freedom as well as working for the freedom of the Exodusters when they worked to make sure the Exodusters completed their journey. Their motivation in helping the Exodusters went far beyond simple charity.

The African American residents of St. Louis knew what the Exodusters were fleeing, because many were themselves migrants who had come to St. Louis from the South. In the decade of the Civil War, the St. Louis African American population increased almost sixfold. In the 1870 census, African American migrants from the South constituted 39 percent of the more than 22,000 African Americans counted. Most of these Southern migrants came from Kentucky, Tennessee, Virginia, Mississippi, and Louisiana. In other words, more than a third of the community that organized aid for the Exodusters had left some of the same Southern states fewer than ten years before. Even politically prominent African American citizens who served on the Exoduster relief committee, the Committee of Twenty-Five, had come to St. Louis from Southern states. The significance of having freedom of movement was not an abstraction to the St. Louis African Americans; it was learned from experience.[33]

When confronted with the Exoduster crisis, the African American community in St. Louis had a number of choices: it could do nothing, it could offer only humanitarian relief, it could insist on sending the Exodusters back to the South, or it could help the Exodusters complete their migration to Kansas. Ultimately, the last option was the one chosen, in many ways the most difficult measure to take. Without an obvi-

33. Christensen, "Black St. Louis," 52–55; Christensen, "The Racial Views of John W. Wheeler," 536.

ous tangible benefit to their own lives, African Americans in St. Louis spent countless hours and funds working to fulfill the Exodusters' desire to leave the South. The benefit, while not obvious, did indeed exist. By helping the Exodusters maintain their mobility, the St. Louis African Americans were taking steps to eliminate Southern bondage once and for all, and were thus reinforcing their own role as a free people in a free society. Although ultimately the Exodus of 1879 did not destroy the system of organized white supremacy in the South, the Exodusters and their St. Louis allies did not passively accept subjugation. Their efforts would live as an example of resistance that would foreshadow the Great Migration of the twentieth century.

In his book *The Story of American Freedom,* historian Eric Foner writes of the importance of the biblical Exodus story to the African American community. Although writing about Dr. Martin Luther King, Jr.'s use of the Exodus story during the civil rights movement, Foner's point applies to the Exodus of 1879 as well. He writes, "Among other things, Exodus suggested that individual rights and group empowerment were interdependent and reinforcing, a point King drove home when he proclaimed, 'we *as a people* will get to the promised land. (Italics mine)'" In writing about the Exodusters, Eddie Glaude, Jr., notes that the "biblical figuralism" of the Exodus story, "articulated a sense of common history and a shared future . . . the uses of the Exodus story solidified that sense of communality needed for conjoint action." Exodus is not only about movement and escape from oppression, it is also about group identity. Using the Exodus story as a metaphor for African American liberation did not begin with the Exodusters, but instead had long been present in African American history. The Exodusters' deliberate connection with this history was not lost on observers of the Exodus of 1879.[34]

Although most Exodusters and their St. Louis helpers were dissimilar in terms of lifestyle, education, and, in some cases, income, their commonality of race was a powerful connection that prompted action by the St. Louisans. Much as the antebellum St. Louis African American elite felt the need to uplift the entire race before the Civil War, the post-Reconstruction elite recognized a tie with the Exodusters. During the Exodus, if the white opposition were allowed to stop the free

34. Eric Foner, *The Story of American Freedom,* 279; Glaude, Jr., *Exodus!* 4; Robert Philipson, "Flight from Egypt: Blacks, Jews, Diasporas," 20; *New York Times,* March 18, 1879.

African American Exodusters from migrating to the West, essentially all African Americans throughout the country would have their freedom limited. After years of slavery and the promise of Reconstruction, losing mobility was unthinkable to both the Exodusters and the St. Louis African American community. The aid for the Exodusters from the African American community in St. Louis was an important piece of the machinery of resistance against the immobilization of African Americans.

Exoduster relief was not solely an African American endeavor, and whites from outside St. Louis played a role in the St. Louis relief efforts. However, it was African Americans themselves who played the most important part, because the African American community had the most at stake. Relieving the Exodusters, and even more importantly, helping them move on to Kansas, was an important piece of the fight against immobilization. The Exodusters were the first large group of African Americans to attempt to move out of the South in the post–Civil War period. Their ability to move unhindered would provide a measurement of the level of freedom available not only to them but to other African Americans as well. Studying the role that the St. Louis African American community took in ensuring the Exodusters completed their journey gives us a prism through which to better understand race relations in St. Louis, as well as African Americans' struggle to maintain their freedom in post-Reconstruction America.

Both Cohen and Painter note that in terms of numbers of participants, the Exodus to Kansas was rather insignificant when compared to the actual African American population. Painter reminds us that "the Kansas Fever Exodus attracted attention completely out of proportion to its actual numbers." Cohen, using census data, determined that just over 25,000 Southern African Americans moved to Kansas during the entire decade of the 1870s. However, the Exodusters' importance was not in their numbers but in their movement, their defiance of a system designed to keep them tied to the land in a posture of subservience. For this reason, the contemporary perceptions of the Exodus and the issues that the movement raised are much more important than the actual numbers of participants.[35]

35. Painter, *Exodusters,* 147; Cohen, *At Freedom's Edge,* 169; Thomas J. Davis, "Another Place, Another Promise, Another Paradise? Another Perspective on Black Migration, Promised Lands, and Paradises," 60.

As Cohen concludes, the Exodus, much like the failed attempts at African colonization that occurred sporadically in the nineteenth century, "were significant because of what they contributed to the cultural and intellectual stream that became black nationalism." A significant characteristic of this philosophy was, in the words of Sterling Stuckey, "a lack of concern for material possessions, and the willingness to risk all in attempting to better the lot of one's people, through revolution or reform." Embedded in this characteristic is a belief in a commonality of values and purpose, and the St. Louis African American community's reaction to the Exodusters reveals elements of pan-Africanism, a concern for all people of African descent. Attempts at migration, even when unsuccessful, made strong political statements and were an important step toward protecting freedom for African Americans by African Americans. As Eddie Glaude, Jr., writes, "The stubbornness of slavery and the persistence of racism warranted recognition that the abolition of slavery did not guarantee freedom (as evidenced in the North). Vigilance of the first order was required of blacks to prevent their return to physical slavery."[36]

Through their own experiences, and through the Exodusters' stories of Southern oppression, African Americans in St. Louis knew that freedom for African Americans was not guaranteed. However, they also were aware that by being in St. Louis at the time of the Exodus, they were in a position to do something. By leaving the post-Reconstruction South for a new life on the Kansas plains, the Exodusters were an example of the lengths that African Americans would go to maintain their hard-won freedom. A thwarting of their attempt to move would be a return, if not to actual slavery, then to hopeless subjugation. When the *New York Times* wrote in a front-page story in April 1879 that the Exodusters' "struggle to make their way to the free West should receive the attention of liberty-loving men and women everywhere," it illustrated the point that the Kansas Exodus represented more than a simple migration to many observers, to the St. Louis African American community, and of course to the Exodusters themselves.[37]

In her book *The Death of Reconstruction,* Heather Cox Richardson observes that the Exodusters became a symbol of free labor for Northern

36. Cohen, *At Freedom's Edge,* 4; Sterling Stuckey, *Slave Culture: Nationalist Theory and the Foundation of Black America,* xi, 45; Glaude, Jr., *Exodus!* 5.

37. *New York Times,* April 3, 1879.

Republicans, whose newspapers contended that the Exodusters were leaving the South to "become free Americans." The Northern Republicans seized upon the Exodus to compare the Exodusters favorably with white Southerners, immigrants, strikers, and communists. Cox Richardson writes that, "As freedpeople appeared to follow the ideal pattern of free laborers, Republicans characterized the actions of white Southerners as an attack on the free labor system. Admiring the African Americans who appeared to take seriously their position as free laborers, Republican observers were predisposed to sympathize with those forced to leave their homes for a better future."[38]

This better future was illustrated in a Thomas Nast cartoon in *Harper's Weekly* that compared the Exodusters to Chinese workers who were being threatened by mobs in California. The caption of the cartoon is "Difficult Problems Solving Themselves," and it encourages the migrations of both oppressed groups. In the drawing, an African American family—man, woman, child, and babe in arms—stand in front of a signpost that reads "To The West." In one hand the man holds a satchel that reads, "A freedman from bull-dozed state," and in his other hand he waves his hat in greeting to a beckoning future. In the western distance are symbols of mainstream America—an American flag, a church steeple, and a WELCOME sign, all waiting for the Exodusters. For all of its promise of a better life, the illustration also reinforced one fact for the freedpeople: they must leave the South to be truly American and benefit from American citizenship.[39]

The Exodusters, like other Americans, understood that they were not truly free until they had freedom of movement to leave the South. Many Exodusters rightly believed that, as post-Reconstruction restrictions on African Americans in the South increased, their ability to leave the South would be compromised. White power in the South was formidable, and was increasing in the wake of Reconstruction's end. The former beneficiaries of slavery worked to solidify conditions that would tie former slaves to the land. As the Exodusters left, they threatened the power structure of the Redeemed South.[40]

38. Cox Richardson, *The Death of Reconstruction,* 163–71.
39. *Harper's Weekly,* March 29, 1879, 256.
40. Cohen, *At Freedom's Edge,* 3.

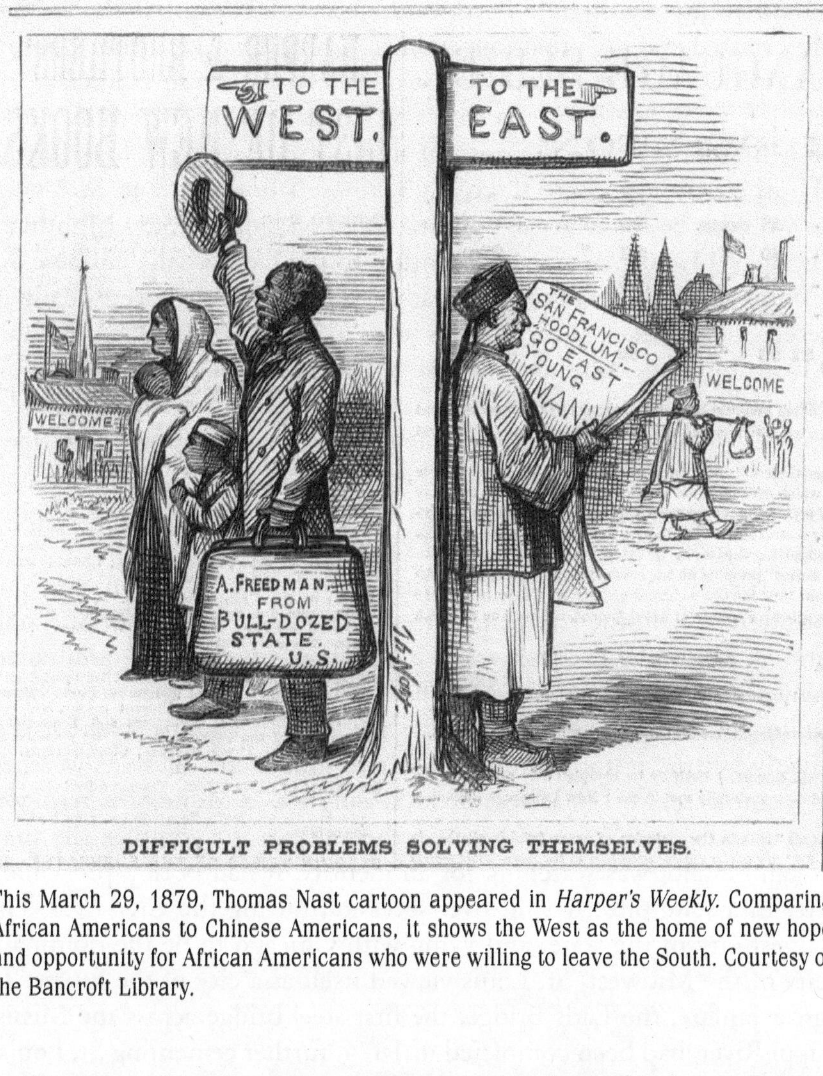

This March 29, 1879, Thomas Nast cartoon appeared in *Harper's Weekly.* Comparing African Americans to Chinese Americans, it shows the West as the home of new hope and opportunity for African Americans who were willing to leave the South. Courtesy of the Bancroft Library.

Southern white planters were increasingly afraid of losing the cheap labor force that the African Americans provided. If too many African Americans left, there would not be enough cheap labor to plant and pick the cotton that provided a substantial part of the South's income. If enough African American laborers left the South, a St. Louis paper editorialized, "the forsaken districts of Mississippi, Louisiana and Arkansas will go untilled this year, and possibly next." The Southern planters, meanwhile, had no way of knowing how many African American laborers would eventually migrate northward, and at the height of the Exodus they started making provisions to bring Chinese workers from California to the South to replace departed African American laborers. One planter, W. B. Murdock, wrote to a St. Louis newspaper from his home in Mississippi, "If the thing is not stopped soon we must look for the 'Heathen Chinese.' Are there any Chinese labor agents in St. Louis, or would it be too expensive getting them on by rail from California?" By April 11, 1879, only one month into the Exodus, the Chinese Six Companies of San Francisco already reported that they were "daily in receipt of applications for laborers to go to the Southern States, notably Mississippi and Louisiana, to take the place of the Negro labor now emigrating." As the potential for massive migration became more widespread, whites in the South became ever more desperate to retain their labor force. This desperation, and the effects it had on the Exodusters and their attempts to pass through St. Louis and continue to Kansas, became more pronounced as the Exodus continued.[41]

If the African American community in St. Louis was in a unique position to help the Exodusters, then, conversely, the city of St. Louis and St. Louis city leaders were in a unique position to be a hindrance. Understanding the city in which the Exodusters found themselves helps us to better understand St. Louis's role in the Exodus. Neither distinctly Northern nor distinctly Southern in attitude, lifestyle, weather, or commerce, St. Louis became increasingly tied to the Southern cotton crop in the 1870s. St. Louis in the 1870s was a complex city that, it can be said, was searching for an identity. It had been a pro-Union city in a state bitterly split over secession during the Civil War. The largest city in the state, and vying with Chicago to be the dominant city of the Midwest, St. Louis viewed itself as a city of the future. To great fanfare, the Eads Bridge, the first steel bridge across the Mississippi River, had been completed in 1874, further cementing St. Louis's place as a key transportation point between east and west. Because of its location at the confluence of two major rivers, its position as a midpoint between New York, San Francisco, New Orleans, and Chicago, and its proximity to the population center of the country, St. Louis leaders were so confident in their city that by 1870 they were proposing that it should supplant Washington, D.C., as the nation's new cap-

41. *St. Louis Globe-Democrat,* April 9, 18, 1879; *Kansas Pioneer,* April 19, 1879.

ital. The St. Louis boosters even held an 1869 convention that included governors and delegates from twenty-one states who pledged their support for the proposal.[42]

Despite its boosters' claims, however, St. Louis was struggling in many ways. The city had suffered economically during the Civil War and had not fully recovered. The war had effectively closed the lower portion of the Mississippi River, and St. Louis essentially suffered a blockade of its most important suppliers. Unfortunately for St. Louis, the same war that had hurt the status of its river economy had boosted Chicago's railroad economy. Chicago, St. Louis's rapidly growing economic rival, was supplanting St. Louis as the most powerful city in the Midwest. By 1878, Chicago was receiving twice as much cattle, six times as much lumber, and three and a half times as much grain as St. Louis, and the discrepancy was growing. The population followed the markets, and St. Louis saw Chicago begin to pull ahead. In the 1870 census, St. Louis census takers had allegedly inflated the city's population by as many as 97,000 people to keep it ahead of Chicago and make it the fourth-largest city in the country, but by the 1880 census such tactics could not hide the truth that St. Louis had fallen behind. The census for that year shows that St. Louis had a population of 350,000 while Chicago was at half a million.[43]

In an attempt to regain its lost status after the Civil War, the city of St. Louis became increasingly tied to the Southern cotton economy, serving as a major Mississippi River shipping point. This relationship would have consequences for the Exodusters, because St. Louis's growth and status were directly tied to the Southern cotton economy, which was dependent upon cheap African American labor. For years, cotton, because of its bulk, was extremely difficult to transport by rail profitably. However, in the early 1870s, James Paramore established several cotton-compressing plants in St. Louis. These plants would compress standard cotton bails into dense blocks only inches high, making railroad transportation much more efficient. St. Louis, because of its railroad connections, had an edge over more Southern ports, and in 1874 cotton receipts exceeded 100,000 bales for the first time. By 1880, St. Louis

42. Parrish, *A History of Missouri,* 217–18; Primm, *Lion of the Valley,* 274.

43. Wyatt Winton Belcher, *The Economic Rivalry between St. Louis and Chicago 1850–1880,* 139–40; Parrish, *A History of Missouri,* 218; Primm, *Lion of the Valley,* 288.

was the third-largest cotton market in the nation behind New Orleans and Savannah, Georgia. Its receipts, which had ballooned to 496,750 bales, made it the largest interior market in the world. This reliance on cotton helps to explain why the St. Louis city government not only tried to discourage Southern African Americans from migrating north but also to encourage those Exodusters already in St. Louis to return to their homes. It became a battle of wits and wills as the city leaders and Southern planters tried to stop the Exodus, and the African American community worked to make sure that the Exodus continued.[44]

Since St. Louis played such an important role in the Exodus, and the responses of its political leaders were so different than those in other cities, it is important to understand the reasons for these differences. St. Louis, "The Gateway to the West," had always been very welcoming of immigrants, but it was officially very unwelcoming to the Exodusters. St. Louis officials first attempted to stop the Exodusters from entering the city, and when that did not work, they tried to discourage the Exodusters from leaving the South, putting the relief efforts squarely on the shoulders of St. Louis's African American community. In essence, when the first Exoduster arrived on the St. Louis levee, this complicated city itself became a character in the Exoduster saga and the Exodusters became a part of St. Louis's history.

44. Katharine Corbett and Howard S. Miller, *Saint Louis in the Gilded Age,* 10; Primm, *Lion of the Valley,* 277–78.

5

The Gateway to the West

I have a wife and nine children along with me.
I have no money to get to Kansas.
—THOMAS CARROLL, EXODUSTER

In the introduction to *Ain't But a Place,* his masterful and touching anthology of African American writing about St. Louis, Gerald Early writes that St. Louis "is more than just a place. It is a presence, a symbol of perseverance, the complex expression of both adversity and victory." Though Early is referring to St. Louis's place in the minds of African Americans throughout its history, his description is particularly fitting in understanding the relationship between the city and the Exodusters of 1879. Escaping their home states and arriving in St. Louis was something of a victory for the Exodusters, but their journey would not be complete until they were beyond St. Louis and settled in Kansas. The Exodusters knew that they needed to pass through St. Louis to get to Kansas, but few realized the adversity they would face in the city. Many of St. Louis's underlying complexities were hidden to the Exodusters in much the same way the city's skyline was obscured by the perpetual coal smoke. Because of its slave-owning past, St. Louis was understood by most Exodusters to be simply a symbol of the South that they were leaving behind, thus one Exoduster's characterization of the city as the Red Sea. Yet St. Louis envisioned itself as a bustling, midwestern city, in many respects separate from the South despite its many connections with the Southern states. This duality of identity informed and affected the way the city and the Exodusters responded to one another.[1]

The Exodusters arrived in St. Louis during a very turbulent era in the history of the city; it was a time of great promise and hope for the future, but it was also a time of great uncertainty. Though its primary rival, Chicago, was growing faster, St. Louis in the 1870s and 1880s was experiencing tremendous growth compared to most cities, and that growth included the African American community. In a twenty-year span between 1860 and 1880, St. Louis saw its population increase more than 100 percent and its geographic area triple in size. Meanwhile, the city's African American population was outpacing the general population—it grew more than six times in size during the same period. African American community institutions attempted to keep pace as schools and churches were added to keep up with demand. Racial and immigration issues, labor unrest, economic problems, political infighting, social concerns, class conflicts, and even geographic changes to the city itself all combined to make Gilded Age St. Louis a very dynamic place. Understanding St. Louis in this era will help contextualize both the Exodusters' plight in the city and the urgency that the St. Louis African American community felt in assisting them.[2]

Gilded Age St. Louis, in the words of historians Katharine Corbett and Howard Miller, "was a place of contrasts and extremes that set progress against poverty, confidence against doubt, and celebration against disappointment." This description of the city as a whole closely mirrors the experience of the Exodusters in St. Louis, and the city's official reaction to their appearance illuminated the complexities of St. Louis's race and class divisions. For the people fortunate enough to be at the top of its hierarchical society, St. Louis represented unlimited potential.[3]

Walt Whitman, who spent three months visiting family in St. Louis in the fall of 1879, just a few short months after the high tide of the Exodus, was utterly charmed by the city. In a writing entitled "St. Louis

1. Early, ed., *"Ain't but a Place,"* xix; *St. Louis Globe-Democrat,* March 19, 1879.
2. Christensen, "Black St. Louis," 108–9.
3. Corbett and Miller, *Saint Louis in the Gilded Age,* 5.

Memoranda" in *Specimen Days,* Whitman praised St. Louis's geography, its wealth, its propensity for commerce, its blending of Old World and New World cultures, and its sense of energy. Whitman also found that St. Louis's orientation, both literal and figurative, between North and South, East and West, was also an advantage. He writes, "It fuses northern and southern qualities, perhaps native and foreign ones, to perfection, rendezvous the whole stretch of the Mississippi and Missouri rivers, and its American electricity goes well with its German phlegm." His description of downtown St. Louis was of a bustling, modern city on the move. He says, "Fourth, Fifth, and Third streets are store-streets, showy, modern, metropolitan, with hurrying crowds, vehicles, horse-cars, hubbub, plenty of people, rich goods, plate-glass windows, iron fronts often five or six stories high. You can purchase anything in St. Louis (in most of the big western cities for the matter of that) just as readily and cheaply as in the Atlantic marts." To Whitman's eyes, St. Louis was not a city looking backward toward the Civil War, but rather was looking to the coming twentieth century when it would continue its ascent as a leading metropolis.[4]

The "Future Great City of the World," as St. Louis booster Logan Reavis billed it, impressed other outsiders as well. A dozen years before Whitman's visit, when St. Louis was still suffering from the effects of the Civil War, the *Atlantic Monthly* featured a story that predicted the city's ascendance as a "greater and more imperial city than Rome" and foresaw St. Louis to be "the future capital of the United States and of the civilization of the Western Continent." A German visitor in 1880 referred to St. Louis as "the London of the American West" because of the growth of its commerce and industry. Mark Twain, visiting St. Louis in 1882 after a twenty-one-year absence, wrote, "the further we drove on our inspection-tour, the more sensibly I realized how the city had grown since I had seen it last; changes in detail became steadily more apparent and frequent than at first, too: changes uniformly evidencing progress, energy, prosperity." St. Louis was a city on the move, looking forward, ready to take its rightful place among the great cities of the world.[5]

4. Walt Whitman, *Specimen Days,* 202.

5. Logan U. Reavis, *St. Louis: The Future Great City of the World,* title page; "The City of St. Louis," *Atlantic Monthly,* 657; Lee Ann Sandweiss, ed., *Seeking St. Louis: Voices from a River City, 1670–2000,* 288; Mark Twain, *Mississippi Writings,* 366.

Visitors often remarked very favorably on St. Louis's commercial strengths, particularly on the natural advantages that St. Louis enjoyed. The city's location, climate, and even its topography all were seen as advantages. One French writer, Louis Simonin, found that St. Louis's topography offered decided benefits in comparison with other American cities. St. Louis, built on a series of gently sloping terraces, had room to expand, unlike New York and Philadelphia, which were both restricted by water, and Cincinnati, which was held back by a bluff. The *Atlantic Monthly* made note of the same geographic characteristic, remarking that St. Louis "can extend itself in every direction back from the Mississippi, without meeting any formidable obstacle."[6]

The city did grow westward from the Mississippi, encompassing the surrounding area. However, a manmade obstacle, the 1876 boundary, eventually stopped the growth of the city proper, leading to the forming of dozens of smaller towns on the city's outskirts. This boundary was created when St. Louis city decided to become an independent entity and separate itself from the surrounding St. Louis County, thus hoping to spare itself the economic drain of the farms on the city's outskirts. This would later prove to be a mistake that would haunt the city as those farms were turned into affluent suburbs. The metropolitan area, unhindered by natural boundaries, continues to grow outward, particularly westward, to the present day.[7]

St. Louis's position on the Mississippi River was, of course, the most obvious natural advantage for St. Louis, and the river was the feature that gave the city much of its character and personality. It was, of course, also the feature that connected St. Louis to the South and made it central to the Exodus. From its founding St. Louis had been organized around the Mississippi River, and as the city grew west, it continued to use the river as an anchor. By 1877, St. Louis stretched eighteen miles north and south along the river. Due to the Mississippi's tributaries, commerce from numerous rivers floated into the city—cotton, coal, grain, lumber, and livestock all passed through and helped St. Louis spread its influence throughout the Midwest and South. However, as

6. Glen E. Holt, "St. Louis Observed 'From Two Different Worlds': An Exploration of the City through French and English Travelers' Accounts, 1874–1889," 68; "The City of St. Louis," *Atlantic Monthly,* 657.

7. Primm, *Lion of the Valley,* 307.

Corbett and Miller note, the river was both a "commercial waterway and yet a bar to overland trade," by hindering East-West shipments. Before the building of the Eads Bridge, ferry rates were expensive, winter conditions often suspended trade across the river, and shipments often needed to be broken down to a more manageable size for transport.[8]

In an 1867 article, the *Atlantic Monthly* noted the difficulties caused by traversing the river. The article states, "At present, it requires seven hundred horses, two or three hundred men, and a dozen large and powerful ferry-boats, to convey across this half-mile of swift and turbid water the passengers and merchandise brought to the eastern bank by the railroads." After the completion of the Eads bridge in 1874, St. Louis—a manufacturing and distribution center—shifted its focus from river trade along a north/south axis to railroad traffic moving east to west. In spite of this shift, the city's proximity to the river was still the defining characteristic and an important factor in the city's growth. St. Louis has been, and always will be, a river town.[9]

Although a discussion of St. Louis economic history is not the purpose of this work, it is important to have some background of the economic changes that shaped the city in 1879, for those changes affected the way the city responded to the Exoduster crisis. Some historians, Wyatt Belcher in particular, view the city's history through the lens of competition between St. Louis and Chicago. In his book *The Economic Rivalry between St. Louis and Chicago 1850–1880,* Belcher argues that St. Louis became too dependent upon river commerce to fully exploit the coming of the railroad and the economic changes that railroads would bring. Belcher contends that St. Louis's natural advantages caused complacency and shortsightedness among business and political leaders who believed that St. Louis was predestined to dominate trade throughout the Mississippi Valley. In his words, "the innate conservatism of St. Louis" was manifested in St. Louis's Southern-bred business leaders, and this conservatism combined with complacency to allow Chicago to emerge victorious as the leading city of the Midwest. In Belcher's view, when St. Louis did finally decide to embrace railroads as an economic tool, it was already too late; Chicago had won the race. Belcher's thesis

8. Ibid., 13–14, 278; Burbank, *Reign of the Rabble,* 2; Lee Ann Sandweiss, ed., *Seeking St. Louis,* 288–89; Corbett and Miller, *Saint Louis in the Gilded Age,* 50.

9. "The City of St. Louis," *Atlantic Monthly,* 655; Burbank, *Reign of the Rabble,* 2–3.

explaining why St. Louis emerged as a loser in an epic Chicago-St. Louis rivalry has been long-lasting and widely accepted in the historical imagination even as both James Neal Primm and Jeffrey Adler have refuted it.[10]

Adler, whose book *Yankee Merchants and the Making of the American West* focuses its argument on antebellum St. Louis, attributes the city's "fall" to neither shortsightedness nor complacency by local leaders. Instead, Adler's book argues that sectionalism, the slavery argument, and an abandonment of St. Louis by Eastern investors who were worried about the strength of slave-holding St. Louis's economic foundation in light of the growing sectional crisis led to the city's "fall." In Adler's view, St. Louis's interest in railroads was an effect, not a cause, of its falling behind Chicago. He argues that St. Louis business leaders not only did not reject railroad development in favor of steamboat development (as is commonly assumed) but that "St. Louis residents embraced the railroad as energetically as did their Chicago counterparts." It was a lack of outside support, not a lack of vision by St. Louis leaders, that relegated St. Louis to second-place status behind Chicago.[11]

Primm agrees, noting that St. Louis first began exploring railroad construction in 1836, not long after railroads were introduced in the United States, and that it was a matter of financing rather than desire that kept the city from developing railroads more quickly. Although he agrees somewhat with Adler concerning the effect of Eastern disinvestments in St. Louis, Primm does not take the argument as far, noting that many Eastern investors stayed in St. Louis even in the midst of the sectional crisis. Primm also does not see St. Louis's inability to keep up with Chicago in as stark terms as Belcher. Instead, Primm gives credit to the St. Louis leadership, arguing, "the failure to keep pace with Chicago should not mask the genius of St. Louis' entrepreneurial leaders in applying its natural, geographical advantages to the material betterment of themselves, their city, and the American West." To Primm, author of *Lion of the Valley,* a book widely recognized as the definitive

10. Belcher, *The Economic Rivalry between St. Louis and Chicago,* 12–15, 206; Eric Sandweiss, ed., *St. Louis in the Century of Henry Shaw,* 134.

11. Jeffrey Adler, *Yankee Merchants and the Making of the Urban West: The Rise and Fall of Antebellum St. Louis,* 7–8, 175–77.

history of St. Louis, the city may not have grown as large or as fast as Chicago, but St. Louis's development is still a success story.[12]

In the years surrounding the Exodusters' arrival, the issue of St. Louis's future was still being decided. The quintessential river town was trying to expand beyond its river roots, and this expansion was causing some growing pains. As the population and activity moved westward away from the river, the former nucleus of the city, the harbor district, became increasingly run-down. Twain notes in his essay the lack of activity on the wharf and the shortage of steamboats and steamboat men compared to the St. Louis he once knew, and he laments the role that railroads played in slowing river traffic. Nicolaus Mohr, a German visitor in 1883, made a similar observation, stating that he was disappointed in St. Louis because its river traffic was not at the level that he expected. Whereas he "had imagined that the water would be covered with Mississippi steamboats, one next to the other, for miles," he instead learned that "these exciting days have passed and today the river is no longer so important. It is the railroads that count."[13]

Raw numbers give credence to Twain's and Mohr's perceptions. In 1877 the Mississippi River carried only 10 percent of the total freight tonnage passing through St. Louis, a severe drop from the 34 percent carried on the river only six years earlier. As riverboat activity dropped, so did economic opportunities on the riverfront. There had always been an African American presence among the river men, even under slavery. Consequently, African Americans had long used the river as a source of economic and geographic mobility, as the Mississippi provided jobs, a way to escape, an avenue to create underground trade networks, and an information system on which news could travel. Although the riverboat traffic dropped and the river no longer carried the amount of freight that it used to, it would carry the Exodusters, who continued the African American tradition of using the river to establish channels of freedom.[14]

12. Eric Sandweiss, ed., *St. Louis in the Century of Henry Shaw,* 114–34.

13. Julian S. Rammelkamp, "St. Louis in the Early 'Eighties," 329; Twain, *Mississippi Writings,* 366; Lee Ann Sandweiss, *Seeking St. Louis,* 352.

14. Philip S. Foner, *The Great Labor Uprising of 1877,* 14; Thomas C. Buchanan, "Rascals on the Antebellum Mississippi: African American Steamboat Workers and the St. Louis Hanging of 1841," 807–8.

By 1879 the focus of activity was no longer on the docks but rather at the entrance to the Eads Bridge, where river traffic, the railroad, and the city all came together to form a vibrant scene. St. Louis, formerly a flourishing yet relatively simple frontier city, was becoming a multifaceted industrial center that its promoters were predicting "would leap into an importance equal to New York and London in an almost incredibly short space of time." Despite his nostalgia for the past, Twain understood that St. Louis was working to take what it saw as its rightful place among leading cities. Describing St. Louis as a "domed and steepled metropolis," Twain wrote that "this solid expanse of bricks and mortar stretching away on every hand into dim, measure-defying distances" had its eye on the future and was striding ever closer toward the twentieth century.[15]

In some areas of life, modernity was already apparent. Within a year of its invention in 1876, telephone service had come to St. Louis, and a few years later fashionable people at the nationally recognized Tony Faust's Oyster House were able to dine on lobster and champagne under the city's first electric lights. A reading of the St. Louis newspapers of the day shows a city following the exploits of the local professional baseball team, patrons attending plays and lectures in beautiful venues, and a population that closely followed national and international affairs. For white citizens in particular, the public education system was innovative and forward-looking. In 1876, British visitor Alfred Falk commented that "the public school system of St. Louis is excellent; the numerous school buildings are commodious, well-ventilated, and many of them really handsome in appearance." Educators gained international recognition as the Hegelian-inspired "St. Louis Movement" infused the public schools and led to the first public kindergartens in the United States. The schools were recognized for their excellence and served as training grounds for educators from cities across the country.[16]

William Harris and other educational leaders pushed for more public access to the democratizing influence of education, and the city's public schools increased from 30 to 103 schoolhouses between 1867

15. Corbett and Miller, *Saint Louis in the Gilded Age,* 51; J. A. Dacus and James W. Buel, *A Tour of St. Louis; or, the Inside Life of a Great City,* 29; Twain, *Mississippi Writings,* 365.

16. Martin Quigly, *St. Louis: The First Two Hundred Years,* book unpaginated; Holt, "St. Louis Observed," 83; Primm, *Lion of the Valley,* 311–25.

and 1881. Harris, a Radical Republican, desired integrated schools, but the idea received little support in St. Louis. The school system was segregated and African American students were relegated to second-class status in their facilities, but in comparison to other former slave-holding cities, St. Louis provided a better education than most.[17]

The successes of the African American schools were due largely to activism by the African American community, which was led by many of the same leaders who would later play a part in the Exoduster relief. Charlton Tandy and other leaders of the Exoduster relief effort were very involved in education issues. One of the most important local issues that Tandy became involved with before he organized the Exoduster relief was in establishing African American schools in St. Louis. Education for African Americans was made illegal in Missouri in 1847 and continued to be illegal until the end of the Civil War, although there had been attempts to circumvent the law.[18]

The most famous case of African Americans finding a way around the law occurred when John Berry Meachum, a free minister and businessman, opened a school for African American children on a steamboat that he had built and anchored in the middle of the Mississippi River. Every morning, Meachum would transport the children to the boat, which was in federal jurisdiction and thus out of reach of Missouri law. James Milton Turner was one of the children who received his early education on Meachum's "floating school."[19]

Churches also served as the homes of secret schools for African American children; both white and African American churches conducted schools in their basements under the guise of Sunday schools and Bible instruction. In 1845, before educating African Americans was technically illegal, a Catholic priest organized a school for African American Catholic girls. At the school, three Sisters of St. Joseph taught elementary classes, catechism, and sewing. However, the authorities pressured the school to close in 1846. After African American education became illegal, sewing classes were often used as a disguise for schools. Elizabeth Keckley, who later grew to fame as Mary Todd Lincoln's

17. Eric Sandweiss, ed., *St. Louis in the Century of Henry Shaw,* 172–73; Christensen, "Black St. Louis," 192.

18. Tandy Papers.

19. Greene, Kremer, and Holland, *Missouri's Black Heritage,* 67–68.

seamstress and confidant, established such a school. The African American aristocracy that was featured in Cyprian Clamorgan's book often sent their children outside of St. Louis to boarding schools. Despite these efforts, before the Civil War most St. Louis African Americans, both slave and free, remained largely uneducated.[20]

During the war, African Americans and their white allies began educating African Americans in the open. In 1863 the American Missionary Society set up a school that served African Americans, most of whom were former slaves, in the Ebenezer Church. Two days after the school opened a mob burned the church to the ground. When the school relocated, its number of pupils swelled to more than one hundred, but at the end of 1863 less than 10 percent of the city's African American children were in school. In 1864, African Americans and sympathetic whites formed the Board of Education for Colored Schools. The board worked with the Western Sanitary Commission, a white liberal organization that was involved in massive relief efforts for freed slaves, to establish nine schools for African Americans. By the end of the war, fifteen hundred African Americans were studying at St. Louis schools.[21]

The law that outlawed African American education was repealed in 1865, and shortly thereafter a law was passed requiring segregated schools for African Americans. African Americans valued education and believed that it was the best way to transfer their newly won freedom into independence and opportunity. Working within the framework of segregation and often facing hostile opposition, Tandy and other African American leaders attempted to build the best possible educational system for African American children. In St. Louis the school board halfheartedly complied with the law and opened three schools for African Americans in 1866. There were 437 African American students in the three schools; they were taught by only seven white teachers. Three years later, 924 African American students from a population of more than 22,000 attended five schools. In 1871, five years after the first schools opened, there were sixteen white teachers in the

20. John A. Wright, Sr., *Discovering African American St. Louis: A Guide to Historic Sites,* 7; Judy Day and James M. Kedro, "Free Blacks in St. Louis: Antebellum Condition, Emancipation, and the Postwar Era," 123–24.

21. Primm, *Lion of the Valley,* 317–18; Day and Kedro, "Free Blacks in St. Louis," 128.

six African American schools. By 1875 the number of African American schools had doubled to twelve.[22]

Although the number of St. Louis African American schools increased, the quality of education remained far below white schools. The segregated schools were separate, but were not equal in terms of funding or location. In 1880, white schools received an average of $39,330 per school, while African American schools received $14,600. African American schools were often in buildings that had been abandoned by whites and that were located far from African American population centers, which forced the children to walk long distances to attend.[23]

The opening of Sumner High School in 1875 is indicative of the school board's attitude toward African American education. The board did not want to open an African American high school and it offered only sporadic high school classes to African American children. After African American parents protested, insisting that their children be allowed to attend a white school to get a high school education, the school board relented and opened Sumner for African American students. The twelve-room building that housed Sumner was formerly Washington Elementary School for white students. It had been deemed unsuitable for white students and abandoned, and had been for sale for six months, but no one purchased it. After the African American parents protested the lack of an African American high school, Washington was renamed Sumner and converted into a combination elementary and high school for African American students. For the African American parents, the feelings of success at having a high school for their children were offset by concerns about the school's physical condition. Since it was located across the street from the Collier White lead works, the air around the school was more polluted than the normally smoky St. Louis air. Because it was a combination elementary and high school, nearly half of all African American students in St. Louis attended the dilapidated, polluted school at Eleventh and Spruce.[24]

22. Thelen, *Paths of Resistance,* 140; Day and Kedro, "Free Blacks in St. Louis," 130; Christensen, "Black St. Louis," 6.

23. Primm, *Lion of the Valley,* 318; Christensen, "Black St. Louis," 119.

24. Primm, *Lion of the Valley,* 318–19; Wright, *Discovering African American St. Louis,* 17; Christensen, "Black St. Louis," 114.

Charlton Tandy and many others in the African American community were angry about the Sumner school plan and called a meeting at the Central Baptist Church. Tandy, who led the protest and the meeting, opened by stating that African American children deserved to attend a clean school in a quiet neighborhood, the same as white children. The proposed school not only sat amidst the pollution from the lead works but also shared a block with a tobacco warehouse and a noisy lumberyard, and it was dangerously close to Union Station and the hundreds of railroad cars that passed through it daily. Tandy also protested the "moral pollution" that existed within two blocks of the school, as many children were forced to walk past the Chestnut Street district of brothels, gambling houses, and saloons to get to Sumner. At the meeting, the superintendent of schools assured Tandy and the others that the school would be sufficient. African Americans continued to hold meetings and protest, but Sumner remained in its location as an African American high school. The protests, though unsuccessful, did show that the African American community was willing to fight for their children's right to a quality education in a safe environment.[25]

After the undeniably mixed success of Sumner High, Tandy and others turned their attention to the classroom, hoping to persuade the school board to hire African American teachers to work in the African American schools. Some African Americans had taught in the African American schools during the Civil War, but until 1877 the St. Louis school board would not hire African American teachers. That year, African American parents staged a boycott of the schools, keeping their children home until African American teachers were hired. The school board capitulated in part because white teachers were protesting being assigned to African American schools, but pressure by the African American community and by African American teachers also played a significant part. The Colored Educational Council insisted that African American teachers "know better the wants of their pupils and how to supply them."[26]

25. Elinore Mondale Gersman, "The Development for Public Education for Blacks in Nineteenth Century St. Louis, Missouri," 37–38; *St. Louis Globe-Democrat,* September 21, 1875; Christensen, "Black St. Louis," 115.

26. Eric Sandweiss, ed., *St. Louis in the Century of Henry Shaw,* 73; Gersman, "The Development for Public Education," 39–40; Thelen, *Paths of Resistance,* 141.

To counteract the school board's contention that it could not hire African American teachers because it could not find any who were qualified to teach classes, the African American community went into action. Meeting in the home of Billy Roberson, a well-known barber and one of the few African American members of the Chamber of Commerce, Tandy and the others devised a plan to find African American teachers. They wrote to African American colleges in the East looking for teachers, and also encouraged friends across the country to locate teachers to come to St. Louis. Lincoln Institute, a Missouri industrial college founded by African American Civil War veterans, also began changing their curriculum to train African American teachers. Richard C. Cole, a Baptist minister, was the first African American teacher hired by the St. Louis public schools. Faced with pressure from African American parents and the reluctance of many white teachers to teach in African American schools, the school board continued hiring African American teachers.[27]

This change in hiring practices dramatically increased the participation of African Americans in St. Louis schools; within the first year after Cole was hired, African American enrollment doubled. Education was viewed as a vitally important tool to possess and a way to advance within a society that set many limits for African Americans. In fact, when compared to whites of similar economic status, African Americans in St. Louis enrolled in greater numbers before school attendance was made compulsory in 1905. Although the African American schools continued to be underfunded, the dedication of the African American community made the schools some of the best in the nation, and African American educational leaders became community leaders. Even though African Americans took pride in their schools, the school board continued to treat their schools in a second-class manner. One example of this was the board's practice of numbering African American elementary schools while naming white elementary schools after distinguished people. In 1878 the Colored Educational Council asked the school board to change the policy and name African American elementary schools after prominent African Americans to serve as an example for students. It was not until 1890 before the board changed the policy. However, a growing demand of African Americans for education meant

27. Young, *Your St. Louis and Mine,* 12; Thelen, *Paths of Resistance* 143.

a need for African American teachers. This need led to the establishment of Harriet Beecher Stowe Teacher's College (now Harris-Stowe State University), a longtime anchor for the St. Louis African American community. The willingness of the African American community to get involved in the education of its children helped to strengthen the community and alleviate some of the strictures of segregation.[28]

In the 1870s, St. Louis was becoming a rather literate city. As a testament to this development, readers in St. Louis were treated to seventy-eight newspapers and periodicals in a variety of languages. Even in the poor sections of town, people read the news religiously. British visitor William Morris noted, "in some of the back slums through which I passed, I had to step over and between the legs of scores of men as they lay in the door-ways of the houses, and on the pavement, reading their newspapers." There were two English-language afternoon papers, eight morning papers—four printed in English and four in German, twenty-three weekly periodicals, including French, Spanish, and Bohemian publications, and an African American publication. These community-based newspapers contributed to building communities among the various populations that were residing together in St. Louis.[29]

The German-language papers were a result of a massive influx of immigration during the middle of the nineteenth century. The first census to make a measure of birthplace, the 1850 census, shows that natives of Germany composed nearly one-third of the population, outnumbering Irish immigrants and even natives of Missouri. The German influence made St. Louis a brewing capital; in 1860 there were forty working breweries in St. Louis. In 1876, St. Louis beer-making became internationally known as Adolphus Busch introduced Budweiser and set up a modern-style supply chain using pasteurization, refrigerated railroad cars, and national advertising campaigns to extend its markets. Beer gardens catering to the city's German population were numerous and provided people a venue to gather, relax, and socialize. In addition to the beer gardens, thousands of St. Louisans socialized at concerts and games in the city's extensive system of parks.[30]

28. Day and Kedro, "Free Blacks in St. Louis," 131; Primm, *Lion of the Valley,* 319; Gersman, "The Development for Public Education," 42; Thelen, *Paths of Resistance,* 143.

29. David Gould, *Gould's St. Louis Directory for 1879,* 43; Holt, "St. Louis Observed," 82; Dacus and Buel, *A Tour of St. Louis,* 536.

30. Eric Sandweiss, ed., *St. Louis in the Century of Henry Shaw,* 83; Primm, *Lion of the Valley,* 329; Corbett and Miller, *Saint Louis in the Gilded Age,* 10–11.

The future crown jewel of the St. Louis parks was Forest Park, which was dedicated in 1876, although at the time of its opening it was still decidedly a work in progress. Containing nearly 1,400 acres along the city's western border, Forest Park was more than 500 acres larger than New York's Central Park and was one of the country's largest urban nature areas. The park's dedication coincided with St. Louis's hosting of the Democratic National Convention, another testament to the city's ambitions. During the dedication ceremony, St. Louis County executive Chauncy Shultz stated that the park was opened so that "the rich and poor, the merchant and mechanic, the professional man and the day laborer, each with his family and lunch basket, can come here and enjoy his own." The park's mission and commitment to democratic ideals reflected a goal to which St. Louis purportedly aspired but often did not attain, especially in relation to the African American community. The park was open nearly a decade before inexpensive public transportation made it possible for the city's poorest families to escape the smoke of the city in the fresh air of the park; before that development a primary complaint was that the park was only accessible to people who could afford to own or rent a carriage. For African Americans, transportation was not the only issue restricting their use of the park. As part of the city's mixed-bag system of Jim Crow laws, areas of Forest Park remained segregated until the mid-1960s, nearly 100 years after its dedication.[31]

Despite its veneer of progress and refinement, the St. Louis that met the Exodusters was still, in many ways, a rough-and-tumble city caught between its frontier roots and its manufacturing present and future. The German visitor Ernst von Hesse-Wartegg noted that despite St. Louis's new wealth, there was also a seamy side that drew visitors from as far away as the Colorado mines and the western range. Coming to St. Louis to cut loose while temporarily escaping their difficult lives on the frontier, the "riffraff," as Hesse-Wartegg labeled them, found plenty of ways to spend their money. To keep the decadence separate from St. Louis's respectable citizens, the western miners and cowboys, as well as the "Mississippi fishermen, mulattoes, sailors and local highwaymen," made use of "a district all their own, of infamous hotels and notorious casinos, saloons and dance halls, and houses of the lowest sort." This

31. Caroline Loughlin and Catherine Anderson, *Forest Park,* 3, 22, 32–33, 194; Selwyn K. Troen and Glenn Holt, eds., *St. Louis,* 127.

sordid side of St. Louis would appear during the Exodus, as some local criminals preyed on the Exodusters. Of course, a few Exodusters willingly dove headlong into the local underbelly.[32]

In his autobiography, *Time of Our Lives: The Story of My Father and Myself,* the poet Orrick Johns describes the seedy aspect of St. Louis that greeted his father upon his arrival in the city in 1883. His account is instructive in understanding the side of the city that was not celebrated. George Sibley Johns, the future editor of the *St. Louis Post-Dispatch,* made it a point as a young reporter to walk the streets and understand the city's personality. His son writes, "Along Chestnut street and Market street the gambling joints and bawdy houses prospered cheek by jowl with doors ever hospitable to friend or stranger. Touts picketed the sidewalks in front of their craps or faro games and openly tipped off the passerby. The girls sat with opulent bosoms in the lace curtained windows, or leaned in the doorways, calling the males, joking, flattering, naming the price." Near the riverfront, on Valentine Street, the scene was even more sordid, as "it contained low-partitioned amorous cubby holes. The girls paraded in front of the flaring doors in a sort of ballet skirt. In and out of them plodded a stream of river men, back from a week's voyage." St. Louis, a "murderous town" and a "complex town of interlocking relationships," was a city where everyone had a prescribed place in the hierarchy; those who moved out of their role would be dealt with. These interlocking relationships—between rich and poor, different immigrant communities, and across racial lines—were constantly a factor in St. Louis life and all impacted the city's reaction to the Exodusters.[33]

In addition to crime-ridden areas, other aspects of life were also a testament to St. Louis's position on the border of refinement and frontier. Twain, for instance, like the Exodusters, made sport of the city's notoriously bad and sediment-filled drinking water, proclaiming that "every tumblerful of it holds nearly an acre of land in solution" while his traveling companion stated that he could drink it "if I had some other water to wash it down with." St. Louis would not have an ample supply of clean, quality drinking water until the early years of the twen-

32. Lee Ann Sandweiss, ed., *Seeking St. Louis,* 289.
33. Orrick Johns, *Time of Our Lives: The Story of My Father and Myself,* 64–65.

tieth century. Aside from the unclean drinking water, in many other respects St. Louis was a dirty city. The streets of the horse-drawn metropolis were fouled daily by twenty-three tons of manure left by the streetcar teams. French visitors commented on the rudeness of the city's residents, observing that the use of chewing tobacco was ubiquitous, and that men constantly spat tobacco juice both inside and outside of buildings. The city skies were black with smoke from the coal that was used extensively by both commercial enterprises and private homes; the smoke was so thick that it stained the walls of buildings, some of them permanently.[34]

The prevalent coal smoke was blamed for causing numerous and often fatal respiratory diseases. Charles Croonenberghs, a French priest who visited St. Louis in 1885, described the city's air quality: "The air is so rich along the Mississippi, the pasty dust from American coal smoke falls so thick in the streets, that one is [as] satisfied by an afternoon walk in St. Louis as if one had eaten a heavy dinner . . . everyone coughs." One reporter for *Harper's New Monthly Magazine* reported in 1884 that the smoke was so thick that "the photographers take their pictures on Sundays, when the chimneys have stopped streaming for the time being, and then some partial prospects are to be had; but as a rule, St. Louis is [as] invisible as London." Despite the breathing difficulties that it caused and the pall that it cast over the city, the smoke that permeated St. Louis was viewed as a sign of progress, evidence of the city's manufacturing prowess. Though its residents were so proud of the city's waste removal system that *Gould's Directory* boasted of "one hundred and eighty miles of sewerage, so arranged and distributed that every acre of territory, every block of the city, finds an easy outlet to the great receptacle for all the filth that accumulates in the streets and alleys," in 1880 less than one-fifth of all homes had flush toilets. This lack of facilities led to tremendous amounts of filth from the outdoor privies. Consequently, the outbreak of disease was always a concern; many residents remembered a cholera epidemic in 1849 that had killed more than 10 percent of the population and forced many residents to escape the city. Another in 1866 had been almost as severe. Dysentery

34. Twain, *Mississippi Writings,* 364; Primm, *Lion of the Valley,* 267; Corbett and Miller, *Saint Louis in the Gilded Age,* 17; Holt, "St. Louis Observed," 78; Lee Ann Sandweiss, ed., *Seeking St. Louis,* 287.

and pneumonia were common; smallpox, malaria, and typhoid fever also killed many people.[35]

In trying to promote St. Louis's image as a healthy city, St. Louis boosters emphasized the city's geographic location, stating, "her geographical position is a peculiarly central one, being located above the miasmatic vapors of the valley, and yet at the foot of the water-shed of the Northwest, giving her a more healthful location than any other city in the world." *Gould's Directory* showed a table comparing the death rate in St. Louis with other leading cities in the country. The table, which *Gould's* states "tells its own story and needs no comment," shows St. Louis to be the healthiest city in the nation by a large margin. St. Louis's death rate of 12 people per 1,000 compares very favorably to the death rates in Memphis (79.22), Chicago (16.49), New York (24.93), New Orleans (50.17), and Washington (26.59), among others. Milwaukee, the second-best city, had a death rate of 14.50, 2.5 people higher than St. Louis. Further examination of the table, however, shows that *Gould's,* like most city boosters of the time, was overly optimistic about St. Louis's population growth, estimating the city's population at 500,000. In actuality, the population in 1880 was only 350,000; when the table was compiled a year earlier it would have been even less. Using the census figure of 350,000, St. Louis had a death rate of 17.00 per 1,000, still lower than average, but not as outstanding as represented.[36]

For those unfortunates who were at the bottom of the city's social hierarchy—including most African Americans in St. Louis—harsh living conditions made simply surviving something of an accomplishment. As Corbett and Miller note, "Gilded-Age St. Louisans generally conceived of their society as a four-tiered hierarchy of the wealthy, the middle class, the working class, and the destitute. They accepted class divisions as facts of life, reflected in personal values, everyday behaviors, and material possessions." Cutting across these lines demarcated by economic class was a hierarchy of race, with African Americans at the bottom. Although a few African Americans were able to overcome

35. Primm, *Lion of the Valley,* 266–67, 340; William Henry Bishop, "St. Louis," 499; Gould, *Gould's St. Louis Directory,* 41; Corbett and Miller, *Saint Louis in the Gilded Age,* 15; Adler, *Yankee Merchants,* 2.

36. Dacus and Buel, *A Tour of St. Louis,* 27; Gould, *Gould's St. Louis Directory,* 41; Primm, *Lion of the Valley,* 272.

some of the effects of St. Louis's racial hierarchy, race was a constant factor that could not be ignored.[37]

Organizations like the St. Louis Provident Association, soup kitchens, and local churches provided basic paternalistic relief for the most destitute St. Louis citizens, with the Provident Association concentrating aid almost exclusively on widows and orphans who were not helped by other agencies. For the year 1878, for example, the Provident Association spent $19,590.25 to help 2,310 families—8,004 persons in all. The Provident Association generally provided basic goods such as coal, bread, flour, and corn meal to the recipients. The association's report does not classify its recipients by race, but it does state that 5,188 of the people helped were "Foreign" and 2,816 were "American." Whether any of the people receiving aid were African American is unknown; in the narrative descriptions of the recipients, race is never mentioned. In an 1878 report, however, the lack of mention of race could lead one to assume that the recipients were Caucasian, although it is an assumption.[38]

The 1879 Provident Association report, submitted at the end of the high tide of the Exodus, makes no mention of the Exodusters and shows that the number of people helped increased by little more than 200 people from the previous year. The Provident Association helped the Exodusters on a very small scale, but it is doubtful that the association played a significant role in aiding many people in the African American community, whether they were Exodusters or St. Louis residents. It was expected that poor African Americans would be taken care of by the African American community. Although the 1878 report stated that a great many of the poor "had been taught to help themselves and others . . . to be sober . . . to be industrious," there was little organized effort from any agency or the government to permanently change people's standard of living. This lack of assistance, combined with a lack of opportunity and choices, meant that many who were at the bottom of the hierarchy would stay there indefinitely. Most African Americans in St. Louis were at the bottom of the hierarchy. Despite the progress made before the Civil War by the "Colored Aristocracy" profiled in Cyprian Clamorgan's pamphlet and the subsequent successes of

37. Corbett and Miller, *Saint Louis in the Gilded Age,* 20.

38. St. Louis Provident Association Record Books 1871–1956, University of Missouri–St. Louis.

a few postwar African American leaders, the vast majority of African Americans in St. Louis found themselves among the working class and the destitute trapped at the bottom of the socioeconomic ladder.[39]

One helpful tool for determining the economic status of African Americans in St. Louis in the 1870s and 1880s comes from the St. Louis schools. School officials recorded the occupations of schoolchildren's parents under eighteen different categories between 1866 and 1894. Of course, there are some limitations to the sample. For one, because of a lack of compulsory education, the children of the poorest parents often were working instead of going to school, so they might not be represented. Another limitation would be that childless workers would not be represented. Finally, it is possible that the schools depended upon the children to report the information of their parents' occupations, thus leading to some inaccuracies. In spite of these limitations, the following information still provides a reasonably accurate representation of African Americans' economic status in 1870s and 1880s St. Louis.[40]

The results for 1876 to 1880, a period encompassing the Exodus, show that African Americans in St. Louis were disproportionately working in unskilled positions. According to the survey, 40 percent of the parents worked as "laborers," and 23 percent worked as "laundresses." The third-largest category, "unclassified," which would include domestics, housekeepers, and servants, was 12 percent. Almost 8 percent of the parents worked as "draymen," 4 percent as "boatmen," and 3 percent as "mechanics" and "farmers." Of the professions that would now be considered white-collar, only the one listed "professionals" had 1 percent of the parents represented. The others, including "agents," "boardinghouse keepers," "clerks," "manufacturers," "merchants," and "public officers," all denoted less than one-half of a percent of the parents. As discussed in the previous chapter, the African American community was well-organized socially, religiously, and politically, but the community as a whole was struggling economically. As Day and Kedro write, "Even the colored aristocracy, wealthy as it was, did not share equal status with the white population. The white Chouteaus made money with

39. *Missouri Republican,* March 20, 1879; St. Louis Provident Association Record Books 1871–1956.

40. Christensen, "Black St. Louis," 161–64.

their money; the black Clamorgans made money with their barbershop." When the Exodusters arrived in St. Louis, they were in desperate need of economic help. The St. Louis African American community, a community working to simply survive economically, would bear the burden of providing the bulk of the economic assistance by tapping into already nearly tapped-out resources.[41]

In St. Louis of the 1870s and 1880s, the poor were not concentrated in any one area. Instead, there were pockets of slums spread throughout the city. St. Louis had developed in a rather haphazard fashion, with the rich and poor oftentimes living in neighborhoods in close proximity to one another. This was not unusual in American cities, and the businesses, homes, and neighborhoods of the wealthy in St. Louis were said to be as fashionable as any in the country. Regardless of the physical proximity between the houses of the rich and poor in St. Louis, however, the symbolic differences were notable. The differences in standard of living were reported to be more pronounced in St. Louis than in many other cities, as "the houses of the poor were meaner, uglier, and more miserable than most, according to local writers and visitors."[42]

African Americans, who accounted for 6 percent of the population in 1880, shared many of these poor neighborhoods with people of German, Irish, English, French, and Bohemian descent. African Americans lived throughout the city, encompassing at least 2 percent of the population in every ward of the city according to 1870 statistics, although a large number of African Americans, nearly 26 percent, lived on St. Louis's near north side. Later in its history, these residential patterns would change, and in 1989, St. Louis would be labeled as one of the most racially segregated cities in the nation, split primarily between largely African American North St. Louis and predominantly white South St. Louis.[43]

According to reports near the time of the Exodus, approximately one-fifth of St. Louisans owned their own homes, leaving the rest of the city's

41. Ralph and Mildred Fletcher, "Some Data on Occupations among Negroes in St. Louis from 1866–1897," 340; Day and Kedro, "Free Blacks in St. Louis,"120.

42. Primm, *Lion of the Valley,* 339; Corbett and Miller, *Saint Louis in the Gilded Age,* 27.

43. Margaret Lo Piccolo Sullivan, "St. Louis Ethnic Neighborhoods, 1850–1930: An Introduction," 75; John E. Farley, "Racial Housing Segregation in the St. Louis Metropolitan Area, 2000."

residents to live in rented houses, boardinghouses, and tenements. The poorest of the residents lived in tenements and alleys that were notorious for their violence and filth. "Clabber Alley," so named because its residents subsisted on the waste milk and clabber that was discarded from the area's dairies, the "Cross Keys," and "Wildcat Chute" were neighborhoods that contained several tenement buildings each. Infamous large dwellings with names like "Castle Thunder," named after a particularly brutal Civil War prison, and "Fort Sumter" fronted on alleys instead of the street and housed numerous people in wretched conditions. These conditions included piles of waste, vermin, little sunlight or fresh air, malnutrition, violence, alcoholism, and a much higher mortality rate than the average population.[44]

One contemporary description of "Castle Thunder" noted the interracial nature of its inhabitants, who occupied what was one of the lowest rungs in the St. Louis hierarchy. It stated, "Taken altogether, this is one of the worst tenement buildings in the city, and its inhabitants are altogether as hard a lot of men, women, and children, of all nationalities and colors, as can anywhere be found. A considerable majority of the crowded population of the 'Castle' are colored people, but white or black, they are alike of the most inferior class. Negro roustabouts, white vagrants, white and black women without decency, live crowded together." Living conditions in the tenement were especially difficult during St. Louis's notoriously hot summers. As the residents looked for ways to mitigate the effects of the heat, they offended the sensibilities of the observers, who wrote, "During the summer the hot stews of evil smells in 'Castle Thunder' are deserted for the top of the house and the little courts and alleys about the locality. Sometimes hundreds of them may be seen, representing both sexes and both the white and the black races, slumbering in promiscuous groups on the housetops, and in the court-yard and alley-ways." Given the desperate nature of the Exodusters, the acute need for housing provided for them by the African American community, and the large African American populations of the tenements, it is conceivable that some Exodusters ended up staying in the tenements while awaiting passage to Kansas.[45]

44. Dacus and Buel, *A Tour of St. Louis,* 412; J. Thomas Scharf, *History of St. Louis City and County from the Earliest Periods to the Present Day,* 166; Burbank, *Reign of the Rabble,* 3–4; Robert V. Bruce, *1877: Year of Violence,* 24.

45. Dacus and Buel, *A Tour of St. Louis,* 413–15.

William Morris, the British visitor, noted that "the women and children in this part of the city are as squalid and dirty as you would find people of the same class in the back slums of an English city." Historian Robert Bruce compares the St. Louis tenement areas of the "Cross Keys" and "Clabber Alley" to tenements in New York, Boston, and Philadelphia, and remarks upon the commonalities. He writes, "In a specimen tenement the bedrooms measured seventy-eight by eighty-four inches, and only six out of the twenty-one bedrooms had windows. Sunlight rarely touched most windows anyway. Many a child knew June as the month when the sun at last reached down to his family's window." Alongside the rats, disease, and other vermin that life in the tenements bred, it would also breed resentment against the inequities of Gilded Age St. Louis society.[46]

Life was scarcely better in the poor, nontenement neighborhoods. One such neighborhood was the "Kerry Patch," a working-class, predominantly Irish immigrant neighborhood made up of squatters who built on land owned by others. Families lived for years in one- and two-room shanties that often had doors broken down and broken windows stuffed with rags to keep out the wind. The residents from the Kerry Patch often worked on the railroads, as laborers in factories, and as police and firemen. They enjoyed strong church connections and access to relatively steady employment, yet they remained somewhat on the fringes of mainstream society as the neighborhood was forced to shift location in the wake of city development. The working poor of the tenements and neighborhoods like Kerry Patch were unsuccessful in challenging economic conditions in St. Louis in the years preceding the Exodus.[47]

Life in the tenements and in neighborhoods like Kerry Patch seemed even bleaker in comparison with life in the wealthier sections of St. Louis. The tenements, in the words of the local newspaper, contained "more crime and misery than all the rest of the town can show." The contrasts between the living conditions of the poor and the wealthy in the city were marked. The poor had, in many ways, been left behind in St. Louis's drive to be a commercial power. As Primm writes, the "hovels, wage cuts, chronic hunger and unemployment, and municipal

46. Holt, "St. Louis Observed," 83; Bruce, *1877*, 23–24.

47. Dacus and Buel, *A Tour of St. Louis*, 417–18; Rammelkamp, "St. Louis in the Early 'Eighties,'" 330; Primm, *Lion of the Valley*, 339.

soup kitchens stood in sharp contrast to the lordly mansions which loomed behind the market, the elegant ladies who descended daintily from their glittering carriages, and the rich merchants and landlords." In contrast to the poor struggling for survival in tenements like Castle Thunder and neighborhoods like Kerry Patch, the lives of the wealthy were luxurious and the homes of the wealthy were palatial. Exclusive areas like Lafayette Square and Lucas Place had Victorian mansions with imported furnishings and the latest amenities, comfortably positioned on quiet tree-lined streets.[48]

Such discrepancies in lifestyle and opportunities caused resentment, and in 1877 that resentment boiled over as St. Louis workers participated in a national railroad strike. In so doing, they organized and implemented the nation's first-ever general strike, essentially paralyzing a major industrial city. The strike became a watershed moment, bringing to the surface the simmering discontent of St. Louis's working class. In addition, it became a moment when African Americans tried to traverse racial lines and use economic grievances to unite with white workers. In the latter half of the nineteenth century, similar attempts were made to politically unite working-class whites and African Americans in areas of the South by using Fusion tickets. Ultimately, both in St. Louis and elsewhere, the white workers chose to unite around race rather than economics. The 1877 strike and the response to it by business leaders would lead to a city firmly controlled by the city's elite. Only two years after the strike, the Exodus would make the issues of race, class, and labor prominent once again.[49]

The strike started on July 17 in West Virginia as a railroad strike, and within a week had spread along the railroad lines to many areas of the country. Railroad workers in the St. Louis area held their first strike meeting in East St. Louis on July 21. Their strike began on July 22; the general strike in St. Louis proper began two days later and lasted for nearly a week. Although the St. Louis strike was part of a larger movement, in St. Louis it reached participation and organizational levels not witnessed in other cities. In other cities the railroad strike moved to other

48. *St. Louis Post-Dispatch,* May 26, 1879; Primm, *Lion of the Valley,* 311; Rammelkamp, "St. Louis in the Early 'Eighties,'" 331.

49. Burbank, *Reign of the Rabble,* 55; Helen G. Edmonds, *The Negro and Fusion Politics in North Carolina, 1894–1901,* 3.

industries; in St. Louis, the strike systematically became a general strike that effectively shut down St. Louis industry. After a rally unified thousands of workers, the railroad workers were joined by factory hands, bakery workers, boatmen from the levee, gas workers, coopers, and even newsboys. The strikers succeeded in closing down at least sixty factories and shops, bringing the St. Louis economy to a standstill. The St. Louis strike, in the words of one historian, "deserves to be recognized as the first exercise in America of labor's ultimate weapon." Like urban laborers who were withholding their labor by taking to the streets, the Exodusters were also striking by leaving the South. In essence, they were withholding their labor because of unsatisfactory conditions. In so doing, they were using one of the few means of power that they possessed.[50]

Because of its wide-ranging locales, the diversity of its participants, and the differing of strike methods (ranging from pitched battles and riots in some cities to meetings and parades in others), there have been many interpretations of the motivation and effectiveness of the 1877 national strike. It has alternately been stated that the strike was a series of riots, simply a railroad strike, a typical labor action, and a socialist insurrection that had the revolutionary potential to create a socialist United States. There are several excellent works that discuss the national strike, including Foner's *The Great Labor Uprising of 1877* and Bruce's *1877: Year of Violence,* but for this work it is particularly important to focus on St. Louis and the effect of the strike on the city. For the strike and its aftermath would help to shape the city's response to the Exodus.[51]

In *Reign of the Rabble,* his book about St. Louis during the 1877 strike, David T. Burbank writes, "In the St. Louis strike, Negro workers made a last gesture of defiance and protest" in reaction to the compromise that settled the 1876 election controversy and effectively ended Reconstruction. Burbank's statement is problematic because the strike was not the last gesture of defiance and protest from African American workers. For instance, if farm workers are to be considered workers, then the Exodus itself can be read as a gesture of defiance and protest against the end of Reconstruction. African Americans also continued in other ways to protest their mistreatment in the post-Reconstruction

50. Philip S. Foner, *The Great Labor Uprising,* 8–9; Thelen, *Paths of Resistance,* 81–82; Burbank, *Reign of the Rabble,* 9–16, 56–58.

51. Burbank, *Reign of the Rabble,* 11.

South. Robin DG Kelley has studied the many means of "everyday resistance" that African American workers employed, including tobacco workers sabotaging production, domestic workers refusing to work, and coal miners pilfering coal to protest work conditions. However, Burbank is correct in noting that St. Louis African American workers played a visible role in the strike, and their involvement produced an intensely negative reaction among many city leaders. This reaction, and the post-strike environment that it created, would adversely affect the Exodusters when they entered St. Louis less than two years later.[52]

In St. Louis, as in other cities, the years leading up to the 1877 strike were difficult ones economically, especially for workers. Starting with the Panic of 1873, the country had suffered through a severe depression. By 1875 unemployment was up to as many as one million people, and many who had jobs only worked part-time. Most workers saw their wages decrease by at least 25 percent between 1873 and 1876, while costs related to living dropped a fraction of that. Railroads were particularly hard-hit; consequently, their employees especially suffered the effects of the economy. As railroads worked to cut costs to balance the difficulties caused by overexpansion and volatility, railroad workers found themselves working more hours for fewer wages. They were also put in increasingly dangerous conditions as crews were gutted and equipment deteriorated; those who were injured on the job were often fired with no compensation. The railroads tightly controlled their workers through Pinkerton muscle squads, and troublemakers were summarily fired. The railroads were able to keep this level of control because national unions were greatly weakened during the mid 1870s, numbering only 50,000 members. The existing railroad unions were largely ineffective in protecting workers' jobs or pay.[53]

In addition to the railroad troubles that were affecting much of the country, St. Louis also went through a banking crisis in the weeks before the strike, watching its oldest bank and others close completely while other financial institutions suspended operations. Combined with monopolization and scandals like the Grant administration's Whiskey Ring (which had deep St. Louis connections), these bank failures had many believing that the nation's new industrial-based economic system

52. Ibid., 7; Kelley, "We Are Not What We Seem," 89–92.

53. Bruce, *1877*, 19; Primm, *Lion of the Valley*, 309–10; Burbank, *Reign of the Rabble*, 7–8.

was on the verge of collapse. Another wage reduction on the Baltimore and Ohio Railroad in West Virginia was finally enough to ignite the nationwide strike that many thought would lead to a social revolution and a purging of the system. In some areas, President Rutherford B. Hayes called out federal troops to protect the status quo, and the encounters between the troops and the strikers turned deadly. In St. Louis the business leaders, police department, and mayor, backed by six companies of federal troops complete with two cannon, eventually put down the strike and arrested the leaders without any loss of life, thus reasserting control over what the elite viewed as their city.[54]

During the week of the St. Louis general strike, few people thought that there would be a peaceful conclusion. After watching thousands of workers participate in parades and rallies with no police control, the British consul reported to London that "the city was practically in the hands of a mob, whilst the inhabitants were in perpetual terror of some outbreak which should exceed in horror the stories that were hourly coming from the City of Pittsburgh." The participants, he stated, were "thousands of the most ignorant and depraved in the community . . . made riotous by the incendiary speeches of their orators." Despite this description, and in fact considering the circumstances, the St. Louis strikers were relatively well organized and very peaceful. The local Workingmen's Party, which quickly assumed leadership over the strikers, made every effort to restrain their more violent tendencies. Ultimately, the refusal of the strike leaders to allow the strike to devolve into class-warfare violence led to its dissolution at the hands of the authorities. At the onset of the strike the Workingman's Party, which contained English, German, Bohemian, and French-speaking sections as a testament to the city's demographic diversity, called for a mass meeting to be held in downtown St. Louis on Monday, July 23. The meeting drew as many as 10,000 people to the Lucas Market where three separate speaking platforms were erected to accommodate the large crowd. It was the first such meeting of labor in St. Louis history.[55]

54. Burbank, *Reign of the Rabble,* 5; Thelen, *Paths of Resistance,* 80–81; David Thelen, "Rutherford B. Hayes and the Reform Tradition in the Gilded Age," 153; J. A. Dacus, *Annals of the Great Strikes in the United States: A Reliable History and Graphic Description of the Causes and Thrilling Events of the Labor Strikes and Riots of 1877,* 386–405.

55. Burbank, *Reign of the Rabble,* 33, 61; Philip S. Foner, *The Great Labor Uprising,* 160–70; Dacus, *Annals,* 377.

Included among the speakers was an African American named Wilson, whose remarks were so well received that he was selected to be one of five men to meet with Mayor Henry Overstolz. At the next night's meeting, also held at Lucas Market and with an even larger crowd, an African American steamboat worker spoke to the crowd about the difficulties of the roustabouts and levee workers, most of whom were African American. He asked the crowd to support the levee workers regardless of color, and the crowd responded with shouts of "We will! We will!" Foner points out that the African American steamboat worker "had good reason to raise the question. Since the end of slavery, neither the trade unions nor the socialist organizations of St. Louis had ever displayed any willingness to cooperate with Black workers, and during its year of existence the Workingmen's Party of St. Louis had not made the slightest effort to recruit Blacks." This encouragement of the crowd to the African American speaker led African Americans to take a very active role in the strike in an attempt to discard a racial yoke as well as an economic one. While rural African Americans were fighting for their rights in the South, their urban counterparts in St. Louis were doing the same.[56]

African American participation in the strike marches of the week led to inflammatory newspaper reports defending the racial barriers that were being challenged. By noting the presence of African American strikers, the newspapers could question the motives and legitimacy of the strike itself. Although the number of African Americans who participated in the strike marches is unknown, to white St. Louis it was distressing that they participated at all. Their visibility during the strike was a challenge to the social order that paralleled and even exceeded the white workers' challenge to the economic order.[57]

African American participation with white workers in the strike was, in the words of one newspaper, a "novel feature of the times." However, most reporters saw more than novelty in the appearance of the African American strikers. The local newspapers appeared to be terrified of them, describing them as "demons," "blood-curdling," "dangerous-looking," and "wild-eyed." J. A. Dacus, a former St. Louis newspaper editor who

56. Philip S. Foner, *The Great Labor Uprising,* 173–81.

57. Thomas M. Spencer, *The St. Louis Veiled Prophet Celebration: Power on Parade 1877–1995,* 17; Burbank, *Reign of the Rabble,* 168.

wrote a widely read potboiler book in the aftermath of the strike, even described African American strikers in apocalyptic terms. About an African American strike leader Dacus wrote: ". . . there was an apparition of darkness, which appeared to all the people. It was not exactly 'Death on the Pale Horse,' but it was a gigantic colored man, mounted on a yellow horse, who led a mob, composed largely of negroes, toward the northern part of the city, for the purpose of visiting and closing the shops, mills, and other manufacturing establishments, in that section of the city. This mob was disposed to indulge in frequent 'ugly yells,' which was well calculated to strike terror into timid souls."[58]

Eventually, the African Americans' prominent role in the strike led the press to blame the Workingmen's Party for giving African Americans the opportunity to upset St. Louis's social and racial values. These accusations, coupled with the inherent racism of the Workingmen's Party, made its leaders cancel any further mass meetings rather than let African Americans participate. After the strike, Albert Currlin, a Workingmen's Party leader, derogatorily stated, "A gang of niggers, it looked like about 500, came to Turner Hall, and sent word that they wanted to join our party. We replied that we wanted nothing to do with them." By canceling the mass meetings that demonstrated the workers' solidarity, the Workingmen's Party leaders were depriving themselves of their most powerful weapon during the strike's most crucial period.[59]

After the mass meetings were canceled, the strike lost momentum and it was merely a matter of days before the city's leaders were back in control. There was plenty of shared blame among the workers for the strike's failure, but as Burbank notes, special blame was placed upon the African American participants. He writes, "In one saloon, an Irishman blamed the Germans and the Negroes for everything. In another saloon, a German blamed the Irish and the Negroes. The English press blamed all the 'foreigners' and, of course, the Negroes. The Negroes must have had their ideas too, but no one paid any attention to them." After the elites regained control over all of the bickering groups, they began taking steps to reinforce the city's hierarchical structure. Since African Americans were, by design, at the bottom of the hierarchy, they

58. Philip S. Foner, *The Great Labor Uprising,* 181–83; Thelen, *Paths of Resistance,* 82; Dacus, *Annals,* 389.

59. Philip S. Foner, *The Great Labor Uprising,* 182.

rightfully believed that the gains that had been made since slavery were imperiled.[60]

The most public method of instructing the public on a need for hierarchy was the Veiled Prophet parade, which took place in October 1878, one year after the strike and just a few short months before the start of the Exodus. Founded by the St. Louis business elite and based upon a New Orleans Carnival Society, the Veiled Prophet organization had the stated goal of attracting visitors and farmers from outside St. Louis to increase St. Louis business by hosting a parade during the St. Louis Agricultural and Mechanical Fair. However, there was another, less stated goal, and that was to assert control over the St. Louis streets in response to the strike of 1877. Five of the Veiled Prophet organizations' original fourteen members had played important roles in ending the 1877 strike, and the parade was a way to show the power that the ruling class possessed. The first parade's Veiled Prophet was the only one whose identity was ever released. It was Police Commissioner John G. Priest, a man who was very visible and very instrumental in ending the strike. The selection of Priest speaks to the class-control aspect of the parade. In addition to overt class control, the parade would be used as a way to educate the parade's mostly working-class spectators in middle-class values and mores.[61]

Each year's parade was organized around a central theme—the first parade, held in the wake of the nationwide conflict between ownership and labor, had the theme of "Festival of Ceres." This parade featured floats topped by Greek and Roman gods, each of whom was advocating different capitalist values. At the end of each parade, the Veiled Prophet (a member of the local elite dressed in an exotic disguise) would appear and be crowned. Other years' parades featured American and St. Louis history, as seen through the eyes of the Veiled Prophet organization. The organization's founding members were born to money and came from St. Louis's leading families, many of whom who had made their fortunes on Southern plantations. The Veiled Prophet members were especially well connected to the St. Louis Merchants' Exchange; nine of the founders served as president during a fifteen-year period. The relationship between the Merchants' Exchange, Southern planters, and the Dem-

60. Burbank, *Reign of the Rabble,* 148.
61. Spencer, *The St. Louis Veiled Prophet Celebration,* 3–27.

The original drawing of the Veiled Prophet appeared in the October 6, 1878, edition of the *Missouri Republican.* Note the similarity in attire to the Ku Klux Klan and the presence of weapons. Courtesy of the Missouri Historical Society.

ocratic party was solidified as the Democrats held their 1876 presidential nominating convention on the Merchants' Exchange trading floor.[62]

The parades showed American and St. Louis history as a story of progress, and especially of progress of great men. The Veiled Prophet members, of course, viewed themselves as the next link in the chain of great men who should determine the direction of the city, the state, and the country. By fostering loyalty to the city and the country in the spectators, the elites believed that they were then fostering loyalty to themselves. Beneath the pomp and the lessons in middle-class values,

62. Ibid., 3–15.

the parades had an undercurrent of violence that showed they were ultimately about power and control. The Veiled Prophet was accompanied on his float by a "villainous looking executioner." Each float in the first year's procession had twenty men surrounding it to keep the crowds at bay, and the newspapers the following day were full of stories of screaming women and terrified children pushed back by the parade and its mounted police escorts.[63]

There was also an element of racial control in the parades. The original representation of the Veiled Prophet, pictured and described in newspapers before the 1878 parade, was of a man in a white robe, pointed hat, and mask. It was reminiscent of the Ku Klux Klan that was growing in the Southern states. The Veiled Prophet carried weapons—a pistol and a shotgun—and had another shotgun within reach. The *Missouri Republican* reported that he vowed not to be stopped "by street cars" or "anything else." Although the representation of the Veiled Prophet had changed by the time of the parade to a less Ku Klux Klan–like image, the connection to racial control was already clear. In the 1882 parade, progress was still the theme, but by then social Darwinism also played an important role as the parade featured "inferior" peoples—Native Americans, African Americans, and other ethnic groups who stood in the way of progress and had to be removed before progress could begin.[64]

The Exodusters would begin arriving in St. Louis less than two years after the 1877 strike had allowed the city's African American workers to demand their rights, and less than six months after a parade to enforce the existing racial and class boundaries suppressed those rights through veiled threats of violence. The St. Louis African American community, faced with the daily challenges of living in St. Louis, would soon be faced with the crisis of helping thousands of others find food, clothing, shelter, employment, and, most importantly, a way to get out of St. Louis. Official St. Louis, itself in the midst of labor, ethnic, and class struggles, would be faced with a crisis of conscience, one that the city would fail. The Exodusters entered a complex city during a difficult time in its history, and the St. Louis African American community organized a relief effort that was vital to ensuring the Exodusters' freedom of movement.

63. Ibid., 4, 33; "The First Veiled Prophet Carnival, October 8, 1878: As Seen by a Contemporary Newspaper," 25–27.

64. Spencer, *The St. Louis Veiled Prophet Celebration,* 6–7, 48–49.

6

Beyond the Exodus

I left the South because I couldn't make a living there, and because we had no rights.
— JOHN MASSEY, EXODUSTER

St. Louis in the post–Civil War era was a symbol of many different things to many different people. People viewed St. Louis through the lens of their own experience, and described the city in terms that fit within the framework of their definition of America. To Logan Reavis and other St. Louis boosters, the "Future Great City of the World" symbolized unlimited promise, potential, and the ascendancy of a new America. To Mark Twain, St. Louis represented the changing frontier, as railroads replaced steamboats, bankers supplanted river men, and respectable businesses replaced barrooms. Walt Whitman saw great things in St. Louis—to him, the growth and promise of the West, and of America, was reflected in the glass windows of St. Louis storefronts. European writers likewise ascribed their preconceived notions of America to St. Louis. To these visitors, St. Louis was simultaneously an industrial city where business and manufacturing occupied every waking moment and also a city peopled by near barbarians who were barely staying ahead of the surrounding frontier.

The Exodusters similarly viewed St. Louis through the prism of their experiences in the South under slavery and during Reconstruction and Redemption. St. Louis, an unwelcoming city in a former slave state, was recognized by the Exodusters as another barrier to cross on their journey toward freedom. The "Red Sea" of St. Louis took on great symbolic significance during the Exodus as the destitute Exodusters languished in the city before making their way to Kansas. St. Louis became a crucible where the strength of the Exodusters' resolve to continue was tested. The city of St. Louis, tied economically to the Southern cotton economy and exhibiting racism that was common to the time, refused to help the Exodusters and attempted to stop the Exodus. The St. Louis African American community recognized that their city was, to the Exodusters, a symbol of slavery and oppression, and the community labored to successfully guide them through the St. Louis barrier. The recently constructed Eads Bridge spanned the Mississippi River to join the East with the West and make St. Louis a vital connection between an older America and a new America. Similarly, the St. Louis African American community served as a bridge moving the Exodusters from their old lives of slavery and oppression to newly found lives of freedom.

To the St. Louis African American leaders who were involved in the Exoduster relief, St. Louis was home. But it was a home with problems, a home where racism was rampant, white business leaders controlled the city, and African Americans were left struggling to ensure that their rights were protected. The Exodus crisis was just one of many events that illustrate their commitment to civil rights and African American freedom during an era of hardening racial attitudes among Missouri whites. There would be different strategies and different battles, successes and failures, but the fight would continue.[1]

Moses Dickson remained involved in politics; he served as a delegate to Republican state conventions numerous times. Despite his involvement in politics and educational issues for African Americans, his tenure as the president of the Exoduster relief committee, and his duties as an ordained Methodist minister, Dickson's principal focus of his energies throughout most of his adult life was on building his fraternal organization. The International Order of Twelve, Knights and Daughters of Tabor was not just a social organization; Dickson envisioned it as a mutual aid society that would provide African Americans the opportunity to support one another morally, financially, and socially—support that was rare for African Americans in a segregated society.[2]

1. Kremer, *James Milton Turner,* 7.
2. Wright, *No Crystal Stair,* 16; Early, ed., *"Ain't but a Place,"* 285.

In the words of Dickson, the members of the International Order of Twelve, Knights and Daughters of Tabor "formed one band, united by the strongest ties of friendship, and bound together by solemn obligations, and established on a firm basis, for the purpose of making a united and effective effort in aiding each member in sickness or distress, to protect and defend each other, to aid and help the widows and orphans of members that died in good standing, to inculcate true morality." The members were encouraged to educate themselves and their children, to live moral lives, to avoid intemperance, and to acquire real estate. Men and women joined Dickson's group on equal terms, but in separate lodges; in some jurisdictions women outnumbered men in the organization two to one. The International Order of Twelve became one of the most successful of the secret societies, growing internationally and continuing into the present day.[3]

Dickson's death in 1901 provided St. Louis with one of the most elaborate funerals ever held in the city. Dickson's burial was held up for nine days in order to give members of the Knights and Daughters of Tabor an opportunity to travel to St. Louis from across the country. Thousands of African Americans and whites visited Dickson's body as it lay in state at his home. At the time of the funeral, thousands of spectators watched as members of the Knights and Daughters of Tabor marched through the streets of St. Louis at midnight to the filled-to-capacity St. Paul's A.M.E. Church. Dickson's body now resides beneath a monument erected in his honor by the Knights and Daughters of Tabor in a cemetery named after him.[4]

For John W. Wheeler, the goal was to carve out a respectable life within the restrictions of St. Louis society. On February 14, 1903, his newspaper, the *Palladium,* listed issues that Wheeler felt were important for the African American community. Under the headline "Something for the Negro to Consider," he wrote: "Organize parents' associations in each school district, to get the idle children in school, to teach cleanliness and manners among them, to break the habit of going from school in droves. Stop loafing around other men's business places. You are in the way. There are 5,000 colored children in the schools and 5,000 out.

3. Early, ed., *"Ain't but a Place,"* 285; David T. Beito, *From Mutual Aid to the Welfare State: Fraternal Societies and Social Services 1890–1967,* 182.

4. Early, ed., *"Ain't but a Place,"* 284; Wright, *No Crystal Stair,* 17–18.

Put those out in. That is our work." Through a mix of social commentary, moral instruction, gossip, and African American economic and political empowerment, Wheeler used the *Palladium* to shape public opinion among African Americans and, at the same time, to change white perceptions of African Americans.[5]

One 1907 column he wrote while bedridden from an accident asks the question, "What Would We Like to See?" The answers to the question contain blurbs that touch on a variety of issues, from political patronage to the price of whiskey. The column says, "A first-class Negro girl that is not likely to be common to all men. Two Negroes in the license department on the monthly pay roll [*sic*] . . . To see the 'Jim Crow' bill in Jefferson City defeated. That will show to the Negroes that the Democrats are not so bad. . . . Fewer mothers who will allow their daughters to keep company with men at 11:30 o'clock at night. . . . A saloon keeper that will give back the right change."[6]

Wheeler became a part-time Methodist minister in 1893, sporadically leading the congregation at St. Paul's as well as other churches in the St. Louis area. Although he ended his ministry when he began editing the *Palladium,* Wheeler continued to call himself the "Political Preacher" and remained interested in the spiritual lives of St. Louis African Americans. The issue of morals runs through many of Wheeler's editorial comments, and Wheeler made particular efforts to warn against the perils that awaited African American women if they did not carefully protect their virtue. As Lawrence Christensen has noted, "Wheeler so often expressed concern about Afro-American women because he believed that they held the future of black Americans in their hands," and the outlook for the future was ominous.[7]

In one editorial, entitled "A Disgrace," Wheeler warned, "There are a number of girls who come home from school and the first thing they do is to go to the butcher or grocery shops and stand and gab with the men in charge. The mothers of these girls ought to be careful, before it is too late. A colored girl should maintain her dignity in her dealings with men in various stores, 'Familiarity breeds contempt.'" Later that some month, a white police officer kidnapped a young African Ameri-

5. *St. Louis Palladium,* February 14, 1903.
6. Ibid., February 2, 1907.
7. Christensen, "The Racial Views of John W. Wheeler," 537–42.

can woman who worked as a servant. To Wheeler, the incident proved that white men only viewed African American women sexually, and that only by maintaining "a dignified and very distant demeanor toward men in general" could African American women prove their virtue.[8]

Young African American women were not the only group singled out by Wheeler for moral instruction regarding activities deemed detrimental to the race. Dark-complexioned African American men, who, in Wheeler's words, "can not get away from their race on account of their blackness, and then will only be seen in company of a yellow girl," were advised to seek help at mental institutions to cure their afflictions. Wheeler was forever concerned that, to the white community, "the lowest type of the negro race is taken as a criterion of all." Therefore, any African American who was, in Wheeler's view, not serving the best interests of the race was liable to be the subject of attacks by Wheeler's pen.[9]

Wheeler was cynical that the color line could ever be fully erased, but he believed that integration was a worthwhile goal. Much of his integrationist feeling was rooted in his Christianity. When an African American minister in Virginia refused to hold funeral services for an African American because a white undertaker had charge of the body, Wheeler was quick to condemn the minister's decision. He wrote, "[the story] displays an unpardonable violation of all laws of Christianity. Rev. Jones ought to remember that God recognizes no color line, and as a minister of the gospel, he shows a very poor conformity to the teaching he advocates." Christianity was a recurring theme throughout Wheeler's views on race. After the death of Lon Williams, a white state legislator and author of a Jim Crow railroad bill, Wheeler questioned what the afterlife had in store for Williams. The *Palladium* story stated, "He is dead now—called by the Maker of All—black, white, red and yellow—to give an account. May the All Merciful Father show more mercy than Williams was willing to give his brother in black."[10]

In keeping with his goals of equal treatment within American society for African Americans, Wheeler opposed African American emigration

8. *St. Louis Palladium,* February 7, 21, 1903.

9. Ibid., November 11, 1905, May 23, 1903.

10. Christensen, "The Racial Views of John W. Wheeler," 541; *St. Louis Palladium,* January 31, November 5, 1903.

to areas outside the United States. When an Alabama senator recommended that African Americans be settled in the newly acquired Philippines, Wheeler responded by arguing that African Americans were better off by staying in the United States. He wrote, "If the American Negro is wise he will remain in the land of his birth. If he acknowledges himself incapable of sustaining the oppression he receives here, when the country has been settled for him, what will be his fate when transported to a country in which the only object is the 'struggle for existence.'"[11]

Wheeler was visible in his leadership and support for resistance against legislated segregation; his newspaper very favorably reported the efforts of Charlton Tandy and other Missouri African American leaders who successfully opposed Jim Crow legislation in Missouri railroad cars in 1903 and 1907. In 1903, John Crisp and Lon Williams proposed legislation that would relegate African Americans to separate cars on railroads in the state. St. Louis African American leaders helped lead the fight against the legislation, and Wheeler was part of a delegation of African Americans from across the state that traveled to Jefferson City to attend the debate of the bill in the Missouri House Committee on Railroads. Charlton Tandy was elected chairman of the delegation, and Tandy, James Milton Turner, and other African American leaders were allowed to testify to the committee.[12]

Their arguments against the bill were well received. Wheeler wrote, "all of the delegates from St. Louis surprised the Committee of Railroads and the entire audience by the commendable display of oratory . . . If those of the House Committee and some of the audience would but acknowledge it, the Negro representatives far surpassed their white opponents." Their oratory helped to carry the day; the bill failed to gain enough support to pass and was defeated by a vote of 55 to 70. Crisp, one of the bill's authors, died a month after the bill was defeated, prompting Wheeler to write, "Missouri loses her strongest advocator for 'Jim Crow' law, and we hope that no other will espire for similar notoriety."[13]

11. *St. Louis Palladium,* January 17, 1903.

12. Christensen, "The Racial Views of John W. Wheeler," 545; *St. Louis Palladium,* March 14, 1903.

13. *St. Louis Palladium,* February 7, March 14, April 25, 1903.

Unfortunately, four short years later, another attempt to legislate segregation on railroad cars was attempted and the issue was again debated. Again, African Americans from across the state marshaled their forces in opposition to the bill. As it had four years earlier, Wheeler's *Palladium* played a key role in publicizing African American support for the bill's defeat. After the bill passed the senate, the *Palladium* was still optimistic that the bill would fail in the house, because the members of the house were more answerable to the people. Tandy again went to Jefferson City with a delegation of leading African Americans, although he did not address the house committee. Across the state, African American churches led prayers against the bill's success, and in the gallery of the house, students from Lincoln Institute sang a rousing rendition of "Nearer, My God to Thee."[14]

When the debate began before the joint committee, the opposition leaders who were chosen to speak proved very able. Wheeler wrote, "The Negroes had a well-planned and cleverly executed program before the committee. There was not a word uttered which could possibly give offense to any white man. The speeches combined wit, eloquence and pathos, and were considered an eloquent plea for the Negro." After the defeat of the bill, Wheeler noted that "both Democrats and Republicans congratulated the representatives of our race and made them feel that all men were not against the race, although they were Democrats." Although still cynical that the color line would ever be fully eradicated, the defeat of the second bill left Wheeler somewhat hopeful. He summed up his hopes by writing, "We have always had the utmost confidence in the brotherhood of mankind, and when the humanity of a man is touched he will turn to the right."[15]

During both fights against the railroad bills, the pages of Wheeler's *Palladium* reflected Wheeler's friendship with Charlton Tandy. Tandy's picture was repeatedly prominently displayed in the paper, and during the 1903 debates, the *Palladium* stated that Tandy was "the best known Negro that is now in the State." Tandy had gained his prominence through decades of hard work, both in local and state politics and in the fight for racial equality. When he was seventy-five years of age, one newspaper wrote of Tandy, "he demonstrates perhaps better than any

14. Ibid., February 9, 1907.
15. Ibid., February 16, 1907.

man in the United States what a negro can accomplish under our form of government."[16]

During his lifetime, Tandy held at least ten appointments from federal, state, and local governments, and worked as an attorney, but it was in his civil rights work that Tandy truly made his mark. He was credited with not only organizing the Exoduster relief and with speaking against legislated segregation, but also with working for educational opportunities for Missouri African American children and with attempting to single-handedly desegregate the St. Louis streetcars. Upon his death, former Missouri state legislator Nicholas Bell said of him, "I knew Tandy for forty-nine years and no man in Missouri has done so much for the Negro race as he."[17]

Working for racial equality was a quality that Tandy learned early in life from his parents; he continued to work for African American civil rights until his death in 1919. To protect African American interests, Tandy organized African Americans to support candidates and use bloc voting. Although his efforts were often successful, especially on the local level, when he died there was still much more work to be done. The headline of the story next to his obituary in the *St. Louis Argus* reads, "Newspapers Plan Lynching Remedy."[18]

The Exodusters' pursuit of freedom was a dramatic illustration of the need for African American equality and it was representative of the civil rights struggle that the St. Louis African American leaders were fighting every day. The Exodusters' journey to Kansas was a repudiation of the reestablishment of white supremacy in the post-Reconstruction South, and for many people, their hegira illustrated the marginal role assigned to African Americans in American society. Despite the gains made by African Americans living in St. Louis, the St. Louis African American community understood that they were among the marginalized and that their freedom was not guaranteed. This understanding reinforced their commonality with the Exodusters, and made them realize that the continuation of the Exodus was a vital issue.

After recognizing the value of the Exodusters' movement, the St. Louis African American community took steps to ensure the Exodusters

16. Ibid., February 7, 1903; Charlton Tandy Papers.
17. *St. Louis Globe-Democrat,* September 5, 1919.
18. *St. Louis Argus,* September 5, 1919.

reached their destination. They understood that if the Exodusters were prevented from leaving the South, or were forced to return to the South, then the freedom of movement of all African Americans would be limited. Any progress that African Americans had made would be threatened. Their work in offering aid to the Exodusters was just one of many ways that they were involved in improving the lives of African Americans. For African American leaders in St. Louis, helping the Exodusters was, in essence, helping themselves.

St. Louis was a complex, hierarchical city, but its African American community had learned to work within the confines of St. Louis society to ease its restrictions against them. Before the Exodus, the St. Louis African American community had led the fight in Missouri to gain voting rights for African Americans, fashion educational opportunities for African American children, create an economic base of African American businesses, establish churches, and resist segregation. Consequently, the organizers of the Exoduster relief were experienced in working for African American civil rights and were also politically connected, and they drew upon these assets when organizing the relief effort.

The effort involved in aiding the Exodusters was immense, as the St. Louis African American community became responsible for feeding, clothing, housing, protecting, and providing transportation for thousands of penniless, displaced persons who felt that they were running for their lives. As word of the Exodus spread and financial and moral support arrived in St. Louis from around the country, the city's African Americans used their existing resources and community connections to organize and distribute the relief. The St. Louis African American churches became barracks, offering hundreds of Exodusters literal and spiritual sanctuary as well as meals, a sense of community, and respite from the weather. St. Louis African American leaders became relief organizers—collecting donations, providing solace, and distributing goods. Most importantly, they became ticket agents, finding passage for the Exodusters to Kansas on the Missouri River packet boats.

The relief effort was not without its conflicts, as old rivalries and different interpretations of the Exodus led to a split into competing organizations. Some established African American leaders, like Frederick Douglass and James Milton Turner, did not recognize the importance of the Exodus and worried that the rural, uneducated Exodusters were a threat to the positive image of African Americans that the two men and others were attempting to cultivate. However, African Americans and their allies across the country, led by the St. Louis African American community, came together to provide the best relief possible for the Exodusters under very difficult conditions. In addition to providing relief, the St. Louis African American community became responsible for publicizing the Exodus—they obtained affidavits to give the Exodusters a forum to tell their story, they wrote letters to newspapers describing the plight of the Exodusters, they held mass meetings to renounce the Southern conditions that had prompted the Exodus, and they met with political leaders to ask for aid. The Exoduster relief effort in St. Louis grew to be about much more than relieving suffering people; it became a movement by African Americans to claim their rightful place within American society.

The Exodus of 1879 was statistically not a large migration; its numbers were dwarfed by the later Great Migration that shifted millions of rural, Southern African Americans to northern cities. The Exodus of 1879 was, however, important symbolically because it was the first large migration by former slaves out of the South. On the last day of 1879 a correspondent from a Chicago newspaper reported, "During four weeks' travel through the State, I estimate the number of colored emigrants at fifteen or twenty thousand. Of these, one-fifth probably are able to buy land, and are making good progress at farming. Most of the others have found, through the Freedmen's Relief Association, places as laborers, and are giving good satisfaction." A year later the *Christian Recorder* reported, "In Kansas, however, the Negro makes very fair progress, and out of the 40,000 who have come to us there are not five hundred receiving aid. Yet more than 30,000 received assistance when they first arrived. Then once they got off the relief associations' hands they never came back, and many of them own homes of their own within two years." At least for a few African Americans from the South, their goals of a new life had been achieved.[19]

In leaving the South, the Exodusters were stating that if freedom was not given to them in the South, they would move and fight to find freedom. This is a theme that is repeatedly reflected within African

19. Haviland, *A Woman's Life-Work,* 486; *Philadelphia Christian Recorder,* December 16, 1880.

American history. Sometimes, as during the Great Migration, the search for freedom involved actual movement from one geographic area to another. At other times, such as during the struggle for civil rights in the 1950s and 1960s, the fight for freedom was less of a geographical movement and more of a movement of the spiritual, social, economic, and political. The St. Louis African American community recognized the importance of the Exodus as a political statement and recognized the Exodusters' worth as human beings who were seeking freedom for themselves and their families. By recognizing this importance, and by working to help the Exodusters claim their piece of freedom, the St. Louis African American community earned its place in the history of the African American freedom struggle.

BIBLIOGRAPHY

BOOKS

Adler, Jeffrey S. *Yankee Merchants and the Making of the Urban West: The Rise and Fall of Antebellum St. Louis.* Cambridge, Eng.: Cambridge University Press, 1991.

Ahlstrom, Sydney E. *A Religious History of the American People.* New Haven, Conn.: Yale University Press, 1972.

Athearn, Robert G. *In Search of Canaan: Black Migration to Kansas, 1879–1880.* Lawrence: Regents Press of Kansas, 1978.

Beito, David T. *From Mutual Aid to the Welfare State: Fraternal Societies and Social Services 1890–1967.* Chapel Hill: University of North Carolina Press, 2000.

Belcher, Wyatt Winton. *The Economic Rivalry between St. Louis and Chicago 1850–1880.* New York: AMS Press, 1968.

Bloom, Khaled J. *The Mississippi Valley's Great Yellow Fever Epidemic of 1878.* Baton Rouge: Louisiana State University Press, 1993.

Bontemps, Arna, and Jack Conroy. *Anyplace But Here.* New York: Hill and Wang, 1966.

Branch, Taylor. *Parting the Waters: America in the King Years 1954–1963.* New York: Simon and Schuster, 1988.

Bruce, Robert V. *1877: Year of Violence.* Chicago: Elephant Paperbacks, Ivan R. Dee, Inc., 1989.

Burbank, David T. *Reign of the Rabble: The St. Louis General Strike of 1877.* New York: Augustus M. Kelley Publishers, 1966.

Christensen, Lawrence O., and Gary R. Kremer. *A History of Missouri: Volume IV, 1875 to 1919.* Columbia: University of Missouri Press, 1997.

Clamorgan, Cyprian. *The Colored Aristocracy of St. Louis.* Edited by Julie Winch. Columbia: University of Missouri Press, 1999.

Cohen, William. *At Freedom's Edge: Black Mobility and the Southern White Quest for Racial Control, 1861–1915.* Baton Rouge: Louisiana State University Press, 1991.

Corbett, Katharine, and Howard S. Miller. *Saint Louis in the Gilded Age.* St. Louis: Missouri Historical Society Press, 1993.

Cox, Thomas C. *Blacks in Topeka, Kansas 1865–1915: A Social History.* Baton Rouge: Louisiana State University Press, 1982.

Cox Richardson, Heather. *The Death of Reconstruction: Race, Labor, and Politics in the Post–Civil War North, 1865–1901.* Cambridge, Mass.: Harvard University Press, 2001.

Dacus, J. A. *Annals of the Great Strikes in the United States: A Reliable History and Graphic Description of the Causes and Thrilling Events of the Labor Strikes and Riots of 1877.* Reprt., New York: Burt Franklin, 1969.

———, and James W. Buel. *A Tour of St. Louis; or, The Inside Life of a Great City.* St. Louis: Western Publishing Company, Jones and Griffin, 1878.

D'Angelo, Raymond. *The American Civil Rights Movement: Readings and Interpretations.* New York: McGraw-Hill/Dushkin, 2001.

Dann, Martin E., ed. *The Black Press 1827–1890: The Quest for National Identity.* New York: G. P. Putnam's Sons, 1971.

Davison, Kenneth E. *The Presidency of Rutherford B. Hayes.* Westport, Conn.: Greenwood Press, 1972.

Du Bois, W. E. B. *Black Reconstruction in America 1860–1880.* New York: Free Press, 1962.

Early, Gerald, ed. *"Ain't but a Place": An Anthology of African American Writings about St. Louis.* St. Louis: Missouri Historical Society Press, 1998.

Edmonds, Helen G. *The Negro and Fusion Politics in North Carolina, 1894–1901.* Chapel Hill: University of North Carolina Press, 1979.

Foner, Eric. *The Story of American Freedom.* New York: W. W. Norton and Company, 1998.

Foner, Philip S. *The Great Labor Uprising of 1877.* New York: Monad Press, 1977.

Glaude, Eddie S., Jr. *Exodus! Religion, Race, and Nation in Early Nineteenth-Century Black America.* Chicago: University of Chicago Press, 2000.

Gould, David H. *Gould's St. Louis Directory for 1879.* St. Louis: David B. Gould, 1879.

———. *Gould's St. Louis Directory for 1880.* St. Louis: David B. Gould, 1880.

Greene, Lorenzo J., Gary R. Kremer, and Antonio F. Holland. *Missouri's Black Heritage.* Rev. ed. Columbia: University of Missouri Press, 1993.

Gutman, Herbert G. *The Black Family in Slavery and Freedom 1750–1925.* New York: Vintage Books, 1976.

Haviland, Laura. *A Woman's Life-Work.* Reprt., New York: Arno Press, 1969.

Henritze, Barbara K. *Bibliographic Checklist of African-American Newspapers.* Baltimore: Genealogical Publishing Company, 1995.

Johns, Orrick. *Time of Our Lives: The Story of My Father and Myself.* New York: Stackpole Sons, 1937.

Johnson, Daniel M., and Rex R. Campbell. *Black Migration in America: A Social Demographic History.* Durham, N.C.: Duke University Press, 1981.

Jones, Jaqueline. *The Dispossessed: America's Underclasses from the Civil War to the Present.* New York: Basic Books, 1992.

———. *Labor of Love, Labor of Sorrow: Black Women, Work and the Family, from Slavery to the Present.* New York: Vintage Books, 1985.

Jordan, Winthrop D. *The White Man's Burden: Historical Origins of Racism in the United States.* London: Oxford University Press, 1974.

Katz, William Loren. *The Black West.* Garden City, N.Y.: Doubleday and Company, 1971.

Kremer, Gary R. *James Milton Turner and the Promise of America.* Columbia: University of Missouri Press, 1991.

Lemann, Nicholas. *The Promised Land: The Great Black Migration and How It Changed America.* New York: Vintage Books, 1991.

———. *Redemption: The Last Battle of the Civil War.* New York: Farrar, Straus, and Giroux, 2006.

Levine, Lawrence W. *Black Culture and Black Consciousness: Afro American Folk Thought from Slavery to Freedom.* Oxford, Eng.: Oxford University Press, 1977.

Loughlin, Caroline, and Catherine Anderson. *Forest Park.* St. Louis: Junior League of St. Louis, 1986.

Lossos, David. *Early St. Louis Area Places of Worship: Chapels, Churches, Missions, and Synagogues.* St. Louis: David C. Lossos, 2001.

Malcomson, Scott L. *One Drop of Blood: The American Misadventure of Race.* New York: Farrar, Strauss, Giroux, 2000.

Masterson, V. V. *The Katy Railroad and the Last Frontier.* Columbia: University of Missouri Press, 1978.

McPherson, James M. *The Negro's Civil War: How American Blacks Felt and Acted during the War for the Union.* New York: Ballantine Books, 1991.

Nieman, Donald, ed. *African Americans and the Emergence of Segregation 1865–1900.* New York: Garland Publishing, 1994.

———. *Church and Community among Black Southerners: 1865–1900.* New York: Garland Publishing, 1994.

Noy, Gary, ed. *Distant Horizon: Documents from the Nineteenth-Century American West.* Lincoln: University of Nebraska Press, 1999.

Painter, Nell Irvin. *Exodusters: Black Migration to Kansas after Reconstruction.* New York: W. W. Norton and Company, 1992.

Parrish, William E. *A History of Missouri: Volume III, 1860–1875.* Columbia: University of Missouri Press, 2001.

Primm, James Neal. *Lion of the Valley: St. Louis, Missouri, 1764–1980.* 3rd ed. St. Louis: Missouri Historical Society Press, 1998.

Quigley, Martin. *St. Louis: The First Two Hundred Years.* St. Louis: First National Bank, 1964.

Rabinowitz, Howard. *Race Relations in the Urban South: 1865–1890.* Urbana: University of Illinois Press, 1982.

Reavis, Logan U. *St. Louis: The Future Great City of the World.* St. Louis: Gray, Baker and Co., 1875.

Sandweiss, Eric, ed. *St. Louis in the Century of Henry Shaw: A View beyond the Garden Wall.* Columbia: University of Missouri Press, 2003.

Sandweiss, Lee Ann, ed. *Seeking St. Louis: Voices from a River City, 1670–2000.* St. Louis: Missouri Historical Society Press, 2000.

Sarna, Jonathan D., ed. *Minority Faiths and the American Protestant Mainstream.* Urbana: University of Illinois Press, 1998.

Scharf, Thomas J. *History of St. Louis City and County from the Earliest Periods to the Present Day: Including Biographical Sketches of Representative Men.* Philadelphia: Louis H. Everts and Co., 1883.

Smith, Henry Nash. *Virgin Land: The American West as Symbol and Myth.* Cambridge, Mass.: Harvard University Press, 1978.

Spencer, Thomas M. *The St. Louis Veiled Prophet Celebration: Power on Parade 1877–1995.* Columbia: University of Missouri Press, 2000.

Stuckey, Sterling. *Slave Culture: Nationalist Theory and the Foundation of Black America.* New York: Oxford University Press, 1987.

Suggs, Henry Lewis, ed. *The Black Press in the South, 1865–1979.* Westport, Conn.: Greenwood Press, 1983.

Taylor, Quintard. *In Search of the Racial Frontier: African Americans in the American West, 1528–1990.* New York: W. W. Norton and Company, 1998.

Thelen, David. *Paths of Resistance: Tradition and Dignity in Industrializing Missouri.* New York: Oxford University Press, 1986.

Troen, Selwyn K., and Glenn E. Holt, eds. *St. Louis.* New York: New Viewpoints, 1977.

Twain, Mark. *Mississippi Writings.* New York: Library of America, 1982.

Whitman, Walt. *Prose Works.* Philadelphia: David McKay, 1892; Bartleby .com, 2000.

Woodward, C. Vann. *The Strange Career of Jim Crow.* London: Oxford University Press, 1966.

Wright, John A. *Discovering African American St. Louis: A Guide to Historic Sites.* St. Louis: Missouri Historical Society Press, 1994.

———. *No Crystal Stair: The Story of Thirteen Afro-Americans Who Once Called St. Louis Home.* Florissant, Mo.: Ferguson-Florissant School District, 1988.

Young, Nathan. *Your St. Louis and Mine.* St. Louis: N. B. Young, 1937.

ARTICLES

Abramowitz, Jack. "The Black Exodus of 1879: A Study in the Origins of Diverging Views in African-American Leadership." *Edutrack,* 2002.

Alston, Lee J., and Kyle D. Kauffman. "Up, Down, and Off the Agricultural Ladder: New Evidence and Implications of Agricultural Mobility for Blacks in the Post-Bellum South." *Agricultural History* 72 (Spring 1998): 263–79.

Anonymous. "The City of St. Louis." *Atlantic Monthly* 19 (June 1867): 655–72.

———. "The First Veiled Prophet Carnival, October 8, 1878: As Seen by a Contemporary Newspaper." *Missouri Historical Society Bulletin* 9 (October 1952): 11–36.

Bellamy, Donnie D. "Free Blacks in Antebellum Missouri 1820–1860." *Missouri Historical Society Review* 67 (January 1973): 198–227.

Bishop, William Henry. "St. Louis." *Harper's New Monthly Magazine* 18 (March 1884): 498–513.

Buchanan, Thomas C. "Rascals on the Antebellum Mississippi: African American Steamboat Workers and the St. Louis Hanging of 1841." *Journal of Social History* (Summer 2001): 798–816.

Christensen, Lawrence O. "The Racial Views of John W. Wheeler." *Missouri Historical Review* 67 (July 1973): 535–47.

Corbett, Katharine T. "Missouri's Black History: From Colonial Times to 1970." *Gateway Heritage* 4 (Summer 1983): 16–25.

Cordley, Richard. "The Advancing Exodus." *Christian Union,* May 14, 1879.

Davis, Thomas J. "Another Place, Another Promise, Another Paradise? Another Perspective on Black Migration, Promised Lands, and Paradises." *Afro-Americans in New York Life and History* 25 (July 2001): 59–67.

Day, Judy, and M. James Kendro. "Free Blacks in St. Louis: Antebellum Condition, Emancipation, and the Postwar Era." *Missouri Historical Society Bulletin* 30 (January 1974): 117–35.

DeArmond, Fred. "Reconstruction in Missouri." *Missouri Historical Review* 61 (April 1967): 364–77.

Dillard, Irving. "James Milton Turner: A Little Known Benefactor of His People." *Journal of Negro History* 19 (October 1934): 373–411.

Douglass, Frederick. "The Negro Exodus from the Gulf States." *Frank Leslie's Popular Monthly* 9 (January 1880). Text obtained through the Electronic Text Center, University of Virginia Library. http://etext.lib.virginia.edu.

Entz, Gary. "Image and Reality on the Kansas Prairie: 'Pap' Singleton's Cherokee County Colony." *Kansas History* 19 (Summer 1996): 124–39.

Farley, John E. "Racial Housing Segregation in the St. Louis Metropolitan Area, 2000." *Edwardsville Journal of Sociology* 2 (2002): www.siue.edu/SOCIOLOGY/journal/FARLEYV2.HTM.

Fletcher, Ralph, and Mildred Fletcher. "Some Data on Occupations among Negroes in St. Louis from 1866–1897." *Journal of Negro History* 20 (July 1935): 338–41.

Garvin, Roy. "Benjamin Singleton and His Followers." *Journal of Negro History* 33 (January 1948): 7–23.

Gersman, Elinore Mondale. "The Development of Public Education for Blacks in Nineteenth Century St. Louis, Missouri." *Journal of Negro Education* 41, no. 1 (1972): 35–47.

Grenz, Suzanna M. "The Exodusters of 1879: St. Louis and Kansas City Responses." *Missouri Historical Review* 73 (1978): 54–70.

Guernsey, F. R. "The Negro Exodus." *International Review* (1879): 378–86.

Hartzell, Rev. J. C. "The Negro Exodus." *Methodist Quarterly Review* 59 (1879): 723–47.

Hier, Marshall D. "Judge Bryan Mullanphy, Brilliant, Benevolent, Bizarre." *Saint Louis Bar Association Journal* (2000). www.bamsl.org/members/barjournal/sum20/Hier.html.

Holt, Glen E. "St. Louis Observed 'From Two Different Worlds': An Exploration of the City through French and English Travelers' Accounts, 1874–1889." *Missouri Historical Society Bulletin* 29 (1973): 63–87.

Hubach, Robert R. "Walt Whitman Visits St. Louis, 1879." *Missouri Historical Review* 37 (1943): 386–93.

Irwin, James R., and Anthony Patrick O'Brien. "Where Have All the Sharecroppers Gone? Black Occupations in Postbellum Mississippi." *Agricultural History* 72 (1998): 280–98.

Kelley, Robin DG. "We Are Not What We Seem: Rethinking Black Working-Class Opposition in the Jim Crow South." *Journal of American History* (1993): 75–112.

King, Henry. "A Year of the Exodus in Kansas." *Scribner's Monthly* 20, no. 2 (1880): 211–18.

Lo Piccolo Sullivan, Margaret. "St. Louis Ethnic Neighborhoods, 1850–1930: An Introduction." *Missouri Historical Society Bulletin* 33 (1977): 64–76.

Moore, N. Webster. "James Milton Turner, Diplomat, Educator, and Defender of Rights 1840–1915." *Missouri Historical Society Bulletin* 27 (1971): 194–201.

Morris, Aldon. "A Retrospective on the Civil Rights Movement: Political and Intellectual Landmarks." *Annual Review of Sociology* 25 (1999): 517–39.

Peoples, Morgan. "'Kansas Fever' in North Louisiana." *Louisiana History* 11 (1970): 121–35.

Philipson, Robert. "Flight from Egypt: Blacks, Jews, Diasporas." *Judaism* 50 (2001): 17–31.

Rammelkamp, Julian S. "St. Louis in the Early 'Eighties." *Missouri Historical Society Bulletin* 19 (1963): 328–39.

Runnion, James B. "The Negro Exodus." *Atlantic Monthly* 44 (1879): 222–30.

Savage, W. Sherman. "The Negro in the Westward Movement." *Journal of Negro History* 25 (1940): 531–39.

Schwendemann, Glen. "The Exodusters on the Missouri." *Kansas Historical Quarterly* 34 (1968): 10–31.

———. "Saint Louis and the 'Exodusters' of 1879." *Journal of Negro History* 46 (1961): 32–46.

———. "Wyandotte and the First Exodusters of 1879." *Kansas Historical Quarterly* 26 (1960): 233–49.

Smith, J. Clay. "Memories of the First Graduates of Howard Law School—1871." Howard University Law School Web site. www.law.howard.edu.

Socolofsky, Homer E. "Kansas in 1876." *Kansas Historical Quarterly* 43 (1977): 1–43.

Strickland, Arvarh E. "Toward the Promised Land: The Exodus to Kansas and Afterword." *Missouri Historical Review* 69 (1975): 376–412.

Thelen, David. "Rutherford B. Hayes and the Reform Tradition in the Gilded Age." *American Quarterly* 22, no. 2 (1970): 150–65.

Van Deusen, John G. "The Exodus of 1879." *Journal of Negro History* 21 (1936): 111–29.

Wamble, Gaston Hugh. "Negroes and Missouri Protestant Churches Before and After the Civil War." *Missouri Historical Review* 61 (1967): 321–47.

Williams, Nudie E. "Black Newspapers and the Exodusters of 1879." *Kansas History* 8 (1985–86): 217–25.

Woolfolk, George R. "Turner's Safety-Valve and Free Negro Westward Migration." *Journal of Negro History* 50 (1965): 185–97.

THESES AND DISSERTATIONS

Christensen, Lawrence Oland. "Black St. Louis: A Study in Race Relations 1865–1916." Ph.D. diss., University of Missouri, 1972.

Gluckin, Morris. "History of the Bryan Mullanphy Emigrant and Travelers Relief Fund." Master's thesis, Washington University of St. Louis, 1946.

Kidd, Florence. "Efforts to Encourage Immigration to Missouri after the Civil War." Master's thesis, University of Missouri, 1933.

PUBLIC DOCUMENTS

U.S. Congress. Senate. Report and Testimony of the *Select Committee of the United States Senate to Investigate the Causes of the Removal of the Negroes from the Southern States to the Northern States.* (Vorhees Committee.) Senate Report No. 693, 1880.

UNPUBLISHED SOURCES

Correspondence and papers of John P. St. John. General sent and received, 17 boxes, 2 volumes; see immigration, Negro Exodus, 1879. Kansas State Historical Society, Topeka.

St. Louis Provident Association Record Books, 1871–1956. Western Historical Manuscript Collection, University of Missouri–St. Louis.

Tandy, Charlton H., Papers. 7 Folders. Western Historical Manuscript Collection, University of Missouri–St. Louis.

NEWSPAPERS

Frank Leslie's Illustrated Newspaper
Harper's Weekly
Kansas Weekly Pioneer
Christian Advocate
Christian Union

Missouri Republican
New York Times
People's Advocate
Philadelphia Christian Recorder
St. Louis Globe-Democrat
St. Louis Palladium
St. Louis Post-Dispatch
Topeka Tribune

INDEX